THE MIDLIST INDIE AUTHOR MINDSET

CONNECT WITH READERS AND CULTIVATE SUCCESS

T. THORN COYLE

Copyright © 2024
T. Thorn Coyle

Cover Art and Design © 2024
T. Thorn Coyle & PF Publishing

Large Print Hardcover ISBN: 978-1-946476-53-1

This book, or parts thereof, may not be reproduced in any form without permission. Nothing here may be used to train Large Language Models, or AI. This book is licensed for your personal enjoyment only. All rights reserved.

Steer your career in the direction you desire. Become the successful author and publisher you want to be... on your terms.

For my Kickstarter backers and everyone who believed in this project as soon as I said I was writing it.

"There's eight billion people on the planet. There are enough people to read what you want to write."
    — Kimboo York

1

MY AUTHOR JOURNEY

I began writing poetry around age five or six, scribbling beneath the orange glow of the night-light in my trundle bed. A precocious reader, I often say that books saved my life. They certainly got me through an often rough, sometimes violent childhood relatively intact.

In my teens and twenties, I wrote, performed, and had poetry published. I penned articles for a local newspaper, wrote for tattoo magazines, and experimented with fiction and plays. I also stalled out on several novels, giving up before ever typing The End.

I pivoted to nonfiction for years, garnering

three traditional publishing contracts and a career that took me all over the world, before finally returning to my first love of novels in 2013, when two characters came knocking, insisting that I tell their story. That was the first novel I ever actually completed. I published it in 2014.

After that, I dove headfirst into learning as much about the craft of fiction as possible, setting a writing schedule and word-count goals, and seriously embarked on indie publishing in 2017 with a four-novel series, The Panther Chronicles.

During that time, I also spent a lot of time and money on courses to help teach me marketing. Those were...informative but not very helpful. First of all, I simply did not have a large enough catalog for that sort of marketing to be very useful. Second, it turns out that the people offering those courses were in the exclusive Kindle Unlimited system but acted as if their methods would work for anyone.

They did not. I'll write more about that in later chapters.

So, I put my head down and kept writing. As my book catalog grew, so did my ability to separate helpful advice from not-so-helpful advice. I figured out how I market, not how other people market.

I began to sell more.

I also turned to crowdfunding in the form of Patreon. This gave me writing practice—I started out offering one essay and one short story per month—and a relatively steady income to supplement my slowly increasing book sales.

As of this writing—exactly ten years after those first characters came knocking—I bring in decent midlist revenue in the high five figures and am heading rapidly toward six figures. This revenue comes from a combination of retail book sales, direct sales of books and merchandise—including Kickstarter—and a combination of Patreon and my newsletter subscriptions. I currently spend very little on advertising—averaging $150 a month, though with increased direct sales from my website, I'll slowly be bumping ad spend up over the next year—and keep my basic business costs minimal, so most of the revenue I bring in is profit.

The information held within the pages of this book is composed of experience from my years of study, examining other successful authors, and figuring out what works for me.

Your path will be slightly different, because your life is different, and your brain and personality are different.

We all must figure out our own way to approach the craft and business of writing. I hope that my journey will offer you some insights into your own.

2

MINDSET FUNDAMENTALS

Mindset is a popular current buzzword. But what are we really talking about when we use that word? One big portion is attitude. That's the core of it. When we change our attitude, we can more readily change our minds. And in changing our minds, it is easier to make changes in our lives.

Now, attitude and mindset are not the only factors at play regarding success, of course. Things such as circumstances, upbringing, imprinting, trauma, systemic support, or systemic oppression impact both how we think and the realities of our lives.

That said, almost anyone can make some changes in their lives beginning with a shift in attitude.

Psychologist and professor Carol Dweck coined the terms "growth and fixed mindsets" in her 2006 book on the topic. A person with a growth mindset believes that things such as skill, talent, or intelligence improve and change with practice. A person with a fixed mindset believes these things are innate. If there's something you aren't good at, you'll never be good at it.

By cultivating a growth mindset, humans are better supported in facing challenges because they believe that they can learn how to face those challenges. People with fixed mindsets tend to be more fatalistic, believing that the deck is stacked either for or against them, and that nothing substantial about their lives will ever change.

Upon examination, we can see how this plays out in our lives. My hope is that this book will help those of us with growth mindsets—what I like to call success, or possibility, mindsets—cultivate even more curiosity about what we can learn next. I hope even more fervently that those of us with fixed mindsets—or what I call defeatist mindsets—begin to find ways to shift our attitude toward greater flexibility and growth.

ACTION: *Ask yourself: Do I currently have a growth or fixed mindset? Why? What are the clues? And is this mindset consistent in all areas of my life, or only a few?*

ASSESSING Where We Are

THE BEDROCK OF DEVELOPING A SUCCESS—OR growth—mindset is deciding what we want and getting out of our own way. Easy, right?

Not really. First, we have to learn to know ourselves well enough to figure out not only *what* we want but *why* and *how*. Not every path is for every person. We all have things we're better at. We all have ways our brains or intuition or skill-building work. We have different personalities affected by all of the above, mixed in with early messages and training.

These differences are all keys to the maps we need to chart our own success.

We'll explore more about what, why, and how throughout the course of this book. For now, let's start with an assessment of our foundations. To cultivate a useful shift in attitude—or mindset—I find it helpful to get the lay of the land, so to speak.

I used to tell my students: "We make magic from where we are, not where we think we ought to be." The less aware we are of our current condition, the more difficult it becomes to make any significant and helpful changes.

So, let's assess where we are before getting into further discussion of mindset.

ACTION: *To begin, take a good look at where you are. Write down your skills—e.g., connecting with people, making graphics, a love of spreadsheets, writing good promo copy—and the things you naturally gravitate toward. Then write down a few areas you might want to study.*

Then, write down what success feels like to you, and write down ten next steps to help you there.

After that? Back up and pay attention to the first step you wrote down. That's where you'll begin.

CURIOSITY AND GENEROSITY

A SUCCESSFUL INDIE author mindset invokes curiosity, generosity, and gratitude, all of which help us as we get out of our own way.

To foster our desired success, we must learn. Learning well requires both curiosity and some measure of determination. Without curiosity, learning is filled with "everyone says to do X, Y, or Z," without pausing to examine *why* or whether that's something we might want to experiment with. Curiosity and experimentation go hand in hand.

Experimentation without curiosity *might* hit success, but might just as easily place us on a map parallel to the one we want to chart. Experimentation without curiosity is not really experimentation at all, it is rote rule-following without questioning who set the rules in the first place.

Curiosity is important because it keeps us engaged with process rather than product. In building success, we need product, but our process is equally key. Too many indie authors do what others suggest without questioning why, and end up unhappy, stressed, or burned out.

Since this book is about building long-term success, we don't want any of that! We need to question both the general *why* and, more importantly, our personal *why*. For example: "Why do I want to put my books into this exclusive subscription service?" Or "Why do I want to run a Kickstarter campaign?"

If I can come up with one to five good answers to that *why* question, maybe it's the right thing for me to experiment with.

This brings me to generosity. Generosity of spirit complements curiosity very well. A generous person listens well, and with interest, and offers what they can in return.

So, one facet of generosity is the recognition that we all have something to offer. Yes, including you.

How many author groups are you part of where someone who joined a week before posts, "Tell me everything you know about marketing"?

Not only is this rude, but it also doesn't take advantage of the group brain trust in any useful way, and is completely selfish. A generous and curious person reads all they can, researches what is on offer, and then, over time, asks useful questions or offers a different perspective.

Those useful questions and perspectives open community dialogue, which is a generous action.

A generous person gives feedback when it is asked for, even if only to say, "I'm new at this, but as a reader, my experience is..." Or, "In my other career, I learned..."

Another way authors are generous to each other is sharing other people's projects, whether it is a new book, a Kickstarter, a blog post, or something else. All that sort of generosity requires is paying attention and spending ten seconds to click a button.

Generous people attract generosity in turn. This is different from self-sacrifice. Self-sacrificing people train others to take and take without giving back. That's the social contract. Generous people are in a power position, rather than a powerless position.

My friend and colleague Katrina Messenger reminds us, "Give only from your excess."

That is what generous people do: they don't give from a place of lack; they give from a position of sharing what they have.

The more generous I'm able to be, the more goodwill is naturally sown, and the more others want to help me. This is not transactional, either.

I'm sure author, podcaster, and industry expert Mark Leslie Lefebvre doesn't think, "Wow, I was generous to Thorn, but what the heck have they done for me?" No. Mark helped me with a free consultation at a very low point in my life—during the worst aftermath of my brain injury—expecting nothing in return but the satisfaction of sharing some knowledge with someone who was struggling.

I'm sure Mark sees the ways in which I attempt to give back to others, but I'm also pretty sure that as long as I'm not actively taking advantage of people, he doesn't care, because generosity is not a quid pro quo operation.

If I'm not talking about transactional, tit-for-tat giving, what do I mean?

It's simple: the energy and attitude of generosity, gratitude, and curiosity breeds more of the same. In this way, what we give out really does return to us.

Celebrating other authors is generosity in action.

ACTION: *What changes in your life will most help you cultivate an attitude of curiosity and generosity? Spend some time with your answers. Meditate on them. Write your thoughts down.*

3

ATTITUDE AND MINDSET

 Useful Attitude

ATTITUDE IS NOT EVERYTHING, not even close. But attitude does affect our relationship to both work and success.

I like to say I am fortunate. For me, fortune is comprised of three things: Circumstance, Effort, and Luck.

Circumstances most certainly affect our success: illness or good health; social connections; financial background; family; education; opportunities; systemic oppression or privilege.... I hope you get the picture.

Let's look at luck next. Luck is the confluence of events that conspire to give a person a boost (or, in the case of bad luck, a fall). Luck is happenstance. Good luck is serendipity. A lightning strike. A lottery win. Some people feel lucky, and others feel unlucky. A lot of that has to do with both attitude and effort, though, which is not luck at all.

There's a famous quote from Thomas Jefferson: "I am a great believer in luck, and I find the harder I work, the more I have of it."

That quote is what I would call a half truth. A lot of people with social and economic privilege —like Thomas Jefferson, who made money off the backs of enslaved people—trot that quote out as proof that it is their efforts alone that have gotten them the successes they enjoy.

This often goes hand in hand with calling successful people "self-made." They are not. No one is. We don't operate in a vacuum, and rely upon all manner of help, education, and opportunities given by circumstance and upbringing.

I would say that successful people are fortunate, not lucky. They enjoy that combination of circumstance, effort, and luck that I am speaking of. It is not that they aren't putting in work, it's just that work is not the only factor in their success.

So, let's examine effort. Effort is the time and energy we put into our relationships, our businesses, and our craft. Effort often makes or breaks a person's success. But not always. Plenty of people work as hard as possible, holding down two or three jobs just to help their families survive, while creating art in whatever spare moments they can find. Those people have it hard, often missing supportive circumstances, or struggling with systemic oppression, or chronic physical or mental illness, or simply lack that nebulous component of luck...or a wealthy family and the opportunities that sort of upbringing affords.

Sometimes, when we're in the midst of struggle, we don't have the time to lift our heads, clear our minds, and gain the perspective that might help us.

So that's another factor in this loose equation: the ability to study and assess what sort of effort is right for us and might be the greatest help in our lives. Cultivating the ability to study and assess our circumstances and surroundings can also require courage. The courage to imagine what might work differently, and to examine the phases needed to shift our current circumstance.

So, regardless of your current circumstances, let's examine different attitudes and how they affect our creative and business lives.

Two Mindsets

There's a lot written about growth mindset versus fixed mindset. To recap: growth mindset posits that our abilities and opportunities can improve through practice and effort. Fixed mindset posits that talent, intelligence, and luck are all set early on and not much we do will change that.

The way children are spoken to often reinforces these two ways of thinking. Telling a child, "You're so smart!" or "You're so nice looking!" reinforces a fixed mindset. Telling a child, "You must have worked hard on that project!" or "I like the outfit you picked today," reinforces a growth mindset. The first tells the child what they are—a comment on their being—while the second tells a child that their being is not linked to their success or presentation.

These concepts are simple enough to understand, and you can likely see what your tendencies are simply by observing your thoughts and language over the course of a fortnight or so.

What I'd like to do now is highlight two mindsets I've personally observed from a variety of creative people over the decades. I call these mindsets Defeatist and Success.

A defeatist mindset tells us we don't have much control over our fate. A success mindset reminds us that not only do we have a great deal of agency, we also have a lot to share.

Two core examples of a defeatist mindset are envy and self-sabotage. There are more variations on this theme, of course, but the following list should get you started with assessing your own thoughts and attitudes.

. . .

DEFEATIST MINDSET:

- *What makes them so special?*
- *They just got lucky.*
- *Their books are terrible.*
- *Readers just want trash.*
- *I'll never make it.*
- *I'm just not good enough.*
- *I shouldn't even try.*
- *I can't do that.*
- *This is too hard. I'll never learn!*

These variations of defeatist mindset only serve to trip us up and keep us stuck. Defeatist mindset is our critical voice, and the voices of shame and self-deprecation, trying to keep us small. It doesn't matter what form the voices take, or what their line of attack is—listening to these voices brings us to the same place: we set ourselves up for frustration and failure.

So, how do we change that mindset to something that feels healthier and more useful?

We examine what those statements are pointing to and ask ourselves what is at the root of the fear that causes us to lean into envy, anger, or self-sabotage. Whose voice, exactly, is speaking inside our heads?

Next, let's explore the counterpart to Defeat, which is Success.

Success Mindset

- *Look at what I get to learn!*
- *I can study one new thing a month.*
- *How can I devote more time and attention to my writing?*
- *What does this person's success teach me?*
- *What if I try...?*
- *I'm curious about how this works.*
- *Let me test that out.*

And, my favorite success mindset phrase, which I coined and return to all the time: *Practice makes possible.*

Action: *What is one mindset adjustment you are willing to work on this week?*

Failure or Success

. . .

WHAT IS FAILURE? Our definition of failure depends on our definition of success, doesn't it? For me, the only real failure is consistently *not* showing up for my stated desires.

If we're steeped in envy or self-doubt, it's hard to muster the courage to try.

Sometimes we give something our all, and it does not come out the way we imagined. Is that failure? No. It simply means that we cannot accurately predict the future. And why is that?

I practice the magical arts, and often say that a divinatory reading is a snapshot of the present and the paths that branch from this moment. As soon as we move, the future changes. Not only do our choices affect the outcome, but so does our interaction with everything around us. We do not create or plan in a vacuum. We co-create.

This is true of every moment and every plan. As soon as I set out a publication schedule, I must simultaneously make a commitment to write. Then I must get a spot on my editor's docket. I either commission art or search through royalty-free sites for images to use in my cover design. Or, if I need to, hire a cover designer to bring the book to life.

I can then decide whether I want to run a Kickstarter or drip the work in progress into a subscription site like Ream or Patreon, or, if I'm this type of writer, a serial site like Royal Road or Vella.

It doesn't matter what sort of career choices I decide on, what matters is my commitment to seeing them through. At least for a while. There is no dishonor in trying something out for a year or two and deciding it isn't the right fit for our career or our audience. I've switched up my Patreon multiple times in the almost decade I've been running one.

Committing to any choice changes both the present and the future, immediately. If I commit to running three Kickstarters per year, that pushes my retail distribution out by several months. That's okay. I can plan that.

If I commit to releasing my work as a serial, I need to think ahead to when I want to publish the work as a whole. Some authors have great success with serial publication platforms and leverage that on Kickstarter before ever thinking about publishing books on Apple, Amazon, Kobo, or in wide print distribution or direct website sales.

That first commitment is life changing because it shapes the next year or two or five of our lives. And how we and our audience respond to and interact with the fruits of that commitment gives us more information on how to proceed further.

There are no correct answers here. There is no one way to set a production, writing, and publishing schedule. There is only the way that works for us, for now. And that's a mindset shift, too. People who embrace diligence and commitment as well as flexibility and experimentation tend toward success.

Your career is in your hands and your effort and attention, your study and practice, help steer your career in the direction you desire.

There will always be outside factors that affect our direction: supply chain issues, algorithmic changes, illness, war.... What we must learn to do is take stock, shift, and adapt. Changing course is easier the smaller your business is.

It's a good thing to be nimble and able to respond to outside influence, including disasters. That said, don't make changes willy-nilly. Stay the course long enough to gather real data and information on what feels right and what sorts of result your efforts are yielding.

Don't be the author who decides to pull their books from publication because initial sales figures feel disappointing. Yes, those authors exist.

Remember: a solid career is a long-term venture. Take a breath, invoke some patience, and then get back to making and executing your plans.

ACTION: *What might you like your author/publisher career to look like? Write down three examples of what an ideal day would include. Next, figure out if there is anything practical you want to add.*

4

PROFESSIONAL INDIE

What's a Professional?

So, you want to be a professional writer...or maybe you already are one, but want to cultivate greater success.

First of all, what is a professional writer? For me, a professional writer is *not* the person who writes one book every three or four years and makes their living with a day job—and yes, consulting, lecturing, and teaching are day jobs. More on that later.

Can you become a professional writer with a day job? Yes. I know many such authors. They manage to write and publish regularly for years and make a steady—even if small—income. This is actually a sound strategy that we'll revisit. Most of these part-time professional authors publish a book or two every year or sell short stories to magazines and anthologies.

If your desire is to become a full-time writer, writing one book every three or four years certainly won't cut it. And in most cases, even one book a year could prove difficult until there's a solid catalog behind it to market. That is not to say that some authors don't make this work earlier in their careers. They do. But most will find it harder to make a living on one book a year.

I want to say right now that there is nothing wrong with being an occasional writer! There is great joy to be found in expressing our creativity and finding ways to share that with the world. As I mentioned already, for years I wrote and published poetry, tried my hand at plays, engaged in some acts of journalism for newspapers and magazines, and practiced fiction, though I never finished one novel I started writing during that time.

I found a lot of joy in this type of writing and publication.

Then I garnered three traditional non-fiction book contracts, spread out over nine years. The first book I sold to New York had a seemingly huge advance that, because of the vagaries of traditional publishing accounting, I still have not earned out. And in reality, it would've been a year's income if you don't factor in my agent's percentage, taxes, and being paid in installments. All of which is par for the course. I supplemented these books with blog posts, essays, poetry, and nonfiction anthology entries. I also wrote and produced four music albums during that time.

Finally, I dove back into fiction and decided to do my best to make a career of it. That meant I needed to study craft as hard as I could, and study the business, and—most importantly—start finishing the novels I'd begun.

Ten years after diving back into the fiction pool, and seven after starting to seriously begin indie publishing, I have a stable career writing both fiction and nonfiction, with a catalog of forty-five independently published titles. These are mostly novels, but sprinkled with thirteen short story collections and four new nonfiction titles.

That doesn't count omnibus editions or professional story sales.

There are romance and mystery authors who make more than I do on far fewer books, and people with slightly larger catalogs than I have not making as much as I do. There are also large numbers of writers whose writing and publishing productivity far outstrip mine, and their income reflects this.

All of that is to say: there's not one way to become a professional writer. We all must find the ways that work for us.

That's what this book is about.

Why Indie?

I'LL GET into some hard numbers in the following chapter, but first, here's an overview of why I appreciate being an independent publisher and author.

The joy of being an independently published author is the autonomy. Is it a lot of work? Sure. But for me, the benefit far outweighs the cost.

As I said in the previous section, I started out as a traditionally published author. At the time, I traveled the world, teaching workshops, hosting a podcast, and doing one-on-one coaching. That was how I made my living. Fortunately, the books and my teaching went hand in hand, boosting each other.

My publishers expected me to do the bulk of the marketing. I had to prove I had a platform. And they licensed all global rights to those three books. It does not matter whether they ever exploit those rights; they own them. They can choose to never license the book in France, for example, or never make an audio version. Or a special edition. These are all options I have for my independently published books because I retain all rights. For those first three traditionally published books? As of this writing, I do not.

Many people still harbor a romantic dream of writing and publishing that has not existed since the 1980s. Mainstream publishers no longer take care of writers. Mainstream publishers no longer issue reasonable licensing contracts. Advances against royalties have diminished hugely, just in the twenty years since I sold my first book to New York.

Very few traditionally published authors can make a living right now, in the 2020s. I can't imagine the situation improving over the next decade, either, considering the bleakness of the current traditional publishing landscape. There are fewer and fewer big publishers out there, and those that remain seem to be gathering as much intellectual property as they can get to pad the bottom line.

When you sign with a mainstream publisher today, most often you sign away all global rights to your own work—foreign licenses, film, audio, and the rest—and are expected to be publicist and cheerleader all while working a second job because your advance will likely not even pay for three months of an average household's expenses. Unless you are one of the lucky few.

On the other side of the publishing fence are the independently published superstars making six and seven figures seemingly out of thin air. A lot of those six- and seven-figure authors exist and are thriving, but getting there is about as easy as garnering a six-or seven-figure contract from a New York publisher. Sure, some people get struck by lightning, but most of us must find our own way to light up the sky.

And some of the six-figure indie authors of just two to five—let alone ten—years ago? They're no longer making six figures. Some of them have slowed down, pivoted, gotten day jobs, and/or are figuring out how to manage a publishing career in new ways. Still others have disappeared from the publishing landscape entirely. They burned out on their pace, or life events arose that impeded their ability to do things the way they preferred, or...the market changed, new readership dried up, and they quit before figuring out how to pivot.

All of that said, independent publishing is my first choice, hands down. I own all the rights to my creations. I can figure out what kind of marketing works for me. I can take a break when I need to, working one hour a day when my energy is at an ebb, or eight-hour days when I have the energy and feel inspired.

I can figure out my best writing pace—four books a year, or six, or two—and figure out how to meet my goals. My average is four novels a year. I also tend to publish two other books a year, either story collections or nonfiction.

Some people write less, and still others write at a far more prolific pace than I, but this works for me. I've got an autoimmune disorder to contend with and had a devastating brain injury a few years back that left me with a disability that limits my screen time and my generative writing capacity.

Instead of letting any of that stop me, I figured out my best schedule and did my best to not compare my output to my more prolific colleagues. By slowly and steadily working, I now have a good catalog of books!

As of this writing, I've slowed down my writing pace to do more experimentation on the publishing side of my business because I now have that healthy catalog to leverage. My business and writing pace will likely change again over time. If I keep a possibility mindset intact, I can make anything work.

One thing I also realized over time is that generating multiple streams of income takes the pressure off book production.

That is important, so I'll repeat it: *Generating multiple streams of income takes the pressure off book production.*

And that's the thing: as an independent publisher and author, I have the freedom to set up as many writing-related business streams as I can manage. I can strategize about how to connect with readers my way. I can experiment and pivot and try new things.

Remember those rights traditional publishers demand? Translation, audio, foreign licensing, film...all of those can become quite lucrative income streams.

As an independent publisher and author, I am in charge of my own business and don't have to rely upon the whims of other people to help my books swim or sink.

I make a comfortable middle-class living.

I've become the fabled midlist author of the previous, more golden decades in the traditional publishing world, but with an important difference:

As an independent publisher and author, I'm making a living on my own terms.

And making a living on my own terms is a mindset all on its own.

ACTION: *Do you want to be—or continue to be—a professional writer and independent publisher? What internal shifts can you make to increase your success?*

5
THE MIDLIST INDIE

What is the Midlist?

EVERYONE WANTS to be an overnight success. Common wisdom is that overnight success often takes at least a decade. Sure, there are folks who hit it big the first time out of the gate, but for most people, slow and steady wins the race.

That has certainly been true for me. I had a successful career before deciding to focus on writing full time, a career that I built over decades.

Add in the fact that because of my minor physical disabilities, I can no longer "do all the things"; the slow build works well for me (I'll talk more about the slow build in a later chapter), as does cultivating multiple income streams, all writing- and publishing-related. This gives me the flexibility I need to build sustainably for the long haul.

In the golden age of traditional publishing—which is long gone, by the way—a midlist author was the bread and butter of many publishing houses. The bestsellers offered the big splashes that kept spirits high and bank accounts flush. The bestsellers also helped bankroll the smallest fish in the pond, the gambles taken that didn't quite pan out because of poor timing, public taste, or any other numbers of factors.

The midlist, though? Those writers chugged along, year after year, earning a decent middle-class living, slowly amassing a catalog of titles, and making a very small name for themselves. They often became known—if anyone remembered their names at all—for a good read that would offer respite from the world. These were the quintessential "paperback writers" who never made it into hardcover but carved out flourishing careers.

Despite early ambitions that included visions of grandeur, that's the sort of author I aspired to be, and the sort I have become.

My writing colleague, science fiction author Blaze Ward once told me, "I'd rather be Bernie Taupin than Elton John."

In case you don't know, Bernie Taupin wrote the lyrics for all of Elton John's greatest hits from 1967 on. So, what I assume Blaze meant was, he wants to work regularly, create marvelous things, make a good living, and not have to deal with the pressure of the spotlight. I agree. That sounds perfect to me.

The midlist attitude also suits our times. The mega hits in music and the bestselling books of twenty or thirty years ago exponentially outstrip the most popular bands and authors of today. We no longer live in a time where almost everyone is talking about the same books, movies, or songs. We may as well embrace this reality and craft a decent living while enjoying our personal journey.

What a decent living is depends on where we

live and how many people we're supporting. I'll write later the importance of cutting expenses where we can, but for many of us, I'd hazard that a middle-class income from writing would be a welcome thing.

So, let's get into some plain talk about money.

What is the Indie Midlist?

For purposes of ease, let's set the bottom of a midlist business income at $50,000 and the top at $150,000. In reality, the new midlist likely starts somewhere around $20,000, which, while a fantastic part-time income that pays a lot of bills, is not a living for most people.

According to *Forbes* magazine, the average US annual salary in 2023 is $59,000. The US Bureau of Labor sets the median earnings of full-time workers at $49,000. So, my number of $50,000 is a good starting point for a midlist author career.

Remember: an average number is the total income number divided by all individual numbers. This means outliers like billionaires and the truly poor are included. A median is the number in the exact middle of all income ranges, so it tends to be a more accurate reflection of salary, instead of being pulled by these outliers.

According to Statista, the two largest percentages of household income in the US in 2022 were 16.2% earning between $50,000 and $75,000 and 16.4% earning between $100,000 and $150,000.

That sounds pretty midlist to me!

The other closest tiers were the $35,000 to $49,000 range at 10.6% of the population, and 12.3% in the $75,000 to $99,999 range.

Let's move on to some other hard numbers, shall we?

According to the Alliance of Independent Authors (ALLi):

In 2022, the median income of self-publishing authors who spent more than half their working time on writing and publishing activities was $12,749.

- The average income was over $80,000.

- Almost a quarter had not yet started to earn, bringing in between $0 and $1K.
- Almost half of the respondents (43.8%) reported over $20k revenue.
- Some 28% earned $50k+ and almost a fifth ran six-figure publishing businesses.

FIGURES from this same ALLi study show that independent author-publishers make far more money than the average traditionally published author, who currently bring in between $6,000 and 8,000 per year. And that figure is on the decline.

This book is for authors wanting to be part of the 28% of indie author-publishers whose businesses make fifty-thousand US dollars and above. This takes time, effort, and strategy, but it is possible to achieve. If I've done it, with all of my issues, you can, too.

What does it take? Steady writing and publishing, for one, plus a good attitude, the ability to study, and most of all, persistence, even when things go wrong.

All of this is where mindset becomes key.

We all have varied circumstances and levels of privilege, but I've often seen people lock themselves into unhelpful patterns, limit their thinking, or simply give up when I really wished they wouldn't.

Shifting our attitudes toward curiosity and engagement is the first step toward midlist success.

But how do we go about this? We assess where we are now and wonder how we got there. Then we look around and study what others are doing and wonder whether that method suits our personality and lives.

Mostly? The successful long-term author doesn't give up.

I'm going to say that again:

The successful long-term author does not give up.

ACTION: *Where are you currently in your writing and publishing career? Are you writing your first book? Have you published five books? Thirty books?*

What is one thing you would like to learn about business, right now?

6

THE IMPORTANCE OF CRAFT

Craft is Business, Too

THIS IS A BUSINESS BOOK, not a writing craft book, but I need to talk about craft because writing is the backbone of our business.

To become midlist indie authors, we need to keep getting out of our own way. Laboring and sweating over one book a year is a great way to put the critical voice in charge and set our creative voice firmly in the back seat. If you work an intense full-time job and write for thirty minutes a day? One book a year plus publishing tasks may be all you can manage. That is fine, and different than the endless polishing that some authors get trapped in. It may just take longer to build a midlist career.

But back to writing: If we need to do research, we research. When it's time to write, we write. When it's time to edit, we edit. It's important to not muddle research and editing into writing, because those activities use different brain functions and can trip each other up.

When the critical voice is in charge, not only does our writing pace slow down, but our stories suffer. We are storytellers, first and foremost. That means that the largest percentage of us are genre writers of some sort or another. Literary writers rarely make a living from writing and publishing. Most of them teach or work other jobs on the side. The exceptions are those literary authors that have mastered the art of storytelling along with their love of language, mood, and tone.

If you want a career as a novelist, genre fiction—pure storytelling—is the way to go. And the best way to learn storytelling is to take in as much of it as you can, via books, films, television, and songs.

The second-best way to learn storytelling is to write as much as you can—and finish what you write—as quickly as you can. Again: the more writing feels like labor, the more our critical voice is in charge.

Back when I labored over one short story a year, writing and rewriting it, my learning of craft stalled out completely. Rather than seeking perfection in one story, I would've been far better served by writing and finishing a dozen or more short stories in that year, learning and improving as I went.

During this time period, I also struggled with the far-too-common fate of many early fiction writers: I quit two thirds into the story—often called the dreaded "mushy middle"—on multiple novels. Looking back, I would have learned so much more if I'd ditched trying to tell the story correctly and simply told a story, any story, *that* story.

Instead, I gave up. I abandoned fiction for years and had to learn all of that upon my return. Luckily, I found some great writing craft mentors, and wrote and wrote and wrote. Over a relatively short time period, I was able to ditch the critical voice in my writing office and start telling (almost) as many stories as my mind could come up with.

Now, if only I had even more time!

Embracing Creative Risk

Point one: We need to become creative risk takers and commit to finishing what we write.

Point two: Allowing our creative voices to take the lead requires practice. I recommend the old Natalie Goldberg advice from *Writing Down the Bones*: set a timer and don't let your hands stop moving until the timer goes off. No editing. No backtracking. Only forward movement while until the timer dings. This is often called the Pomodoro technique, developed by Francesco Cirillo when he was a student who needed to focus! He started ten minutes at a time. During the worst of my brain injury, an occupational therapist recommended the same. I was to do all tasks for ten minutes, then take a break. This worked for my business and writing. I have since worked up to the more standard twenty-minute sprint.

Sprinting practice frees us up from the perfectionist inside our heads that always wants us to do things the *right* way instead of the way that feels most natural to our creative spirits.

Suggestion: After you take a short stretch break and a sip of water, cycle back and skim over what you wrote last, adding details and threading in missed plot points. But don't let your inner critic take over here! You're still in creative voice. Writing is still play.

Once you've quickly cycled through the previous two to six hundred words, press the timer button and go for another twenty-minute sprint.

Figure out how to make this work for you. Some writers thrive on the bustle of a café while writing. Others need to tune out as many distractions as possible. As a neurodivergent person, I write best when I slip earbuds in and put a song on continuous loop, sound turned low. That short circuits the part of my brain that wants to get distracted—it's kept busy by the repetitive music—allowing my creative voice to come to the forefront and create characters, worlds, and words.

If you've never tried timed sprints before, after a week or two, I bet you'll be amazed at how easy it is to enter a flow state. The more we are in the flow, the more our creativity comes out to play, and the more books we can write because our critical voice isn't stopping us all the time to tell us what we are doing is wrong.

Writer Dean Wesley Smith reminds us that story setting all comes from character opinion. As a reader, I can now tell when a writer is making up setting description rather than allowing it to emerge through the character's thoughts and voice. It throws me out of the story.

So, how do I practice character opinion?

What I like to do is to take a breath, drop into my point-of-view character's head, and only then press that timer button. From inside the character's head—be they human, corgi, cat, dragon, or elf—I am awash in sensory information. What am I, as the character, feeling, seeing, hearing, tasting, touching, smelling, or otherwise sensing? That all goes onto the page.

All of that detail becomes natural the more

we practice. We no longer have to think, "Wait, do I have enough sensory detail in this scene?" because we're *in* the scene, inside our character's head.

You'll be amazed how much world building arises on its own because of this, how much information you'll get about the other characters and their cultures, and what surprising plot turns will emerge, simply by letting your main character move through the world.

We build worlds not by planning out every detail, but by letting the experiences of our point-of-view characters set the scene.

I confess that I am a discovery writer, not an outliner. I might do some research or mild brainstorming about a series before I start writing—usually while I'm working on a different series altogether—but I don't spend months or years tinkering with the details.

That said, even outliners can use this method to increase both craft and speed. If you're an outliner, quickly look at your notes on the next scene, then...take a breath, drop into your point of view character's head, set a timer for twenty minutes, and type without stopping!

This method can take some getting used to. The critical parts that want to be in control and tell us we're doing it wrong might put up resistance at first. But I guarantee that the more you practice this method, the freer and more engaging your writing will become.

You know what that means?

Your storytelling will improve, your readers will be happier, and you'll sell more books and have greater series read through. You'll also sell more books because you'll be able to write and publish more quickly, which increases discoverability.

Once you get used to dropping into character and writing away, you can study other craft techniques—like reading T. Taylor's *7 Figure Fiction* or Zoe York's *Romancing the Beat*, or watching Brandon Sanderson's YouTube lectures on science fiction and fantasy world building—and let all that thinking about craft filter toward the back of your brain.

Let yourself practice. Have fun! Do some writing exercises.

Then take what you've been practicing and start to weave that into your timed sprints. Allow what entered through the front of your brain and filtered into the back of your brain to exit through your fingers without really thinking about it anymore.

Beginning writers worry about their books all the time. They seek perfection, and work and work to get as close to that as possible. Beginning writers don't yet trust the process and keep themselves at arm's length from the story, attempting to play puppet master and control things from outside.

That's a natural phase. Every artist is clunky while learning their craft. But artists who become successful for the long run all have deep relationships with art and craft, with their materials and their practice.

Successful artists with satisfying careers all allow themselves to get lost in their creations.

That's the key: let your storytelling become immersive *for you*. The more we can let go of rational control, the more our creative voice will bring our characters to life.

If storytelling is immersive as we write the book, our readers are far more likely to become immersed themselves.

Immersed readers fall in love with our worlds, our stories, and our characters. It does not matter what genre we write in: a reader in love will keep coming back for more.

ACTION: *What do you enjoy most about writing? How can you foster that enjoyment?*

Make some time to study craft. Read books, take classes, or just pick a technique and spend thirty minutes practicing it a week. But when it comes time to write the next book?

Dive into your world and just write.

7

LETTING GO OF WHAT'S TOXIC

Moving Away From Toxic People

THERE'S a mindset shift some of us need to make regarding the people we surround ourselves with. Sadly, we may have to go it alone for a while before finding supportive people better attuned to their own desires. But supportive people are out there, and despite some of the toxicity in online spaces, the Internet hosts a wealth of generous writers happy to share information and cheer others on.

Despite generosity not being a quid pro quo operation, we need to have peers and mentors who feed us. We need people around us whom we can learn from and others whom we can share information, troubles, and successes with.

If what we are giving out isn't returning to us in tangible ways, that is often a sign that we need to link up with a healthier community.

There are toxic people in the world. Or, better said, people who are toxic to us. It doesn't mean they are bad people. We might even like them! Sort of like the way I enjoy peppers and tomatoes even though they give me brain fog and slow me down.

The joys of my autoimmune disorder aside, my mindset around this lies in the answer to these sorts of questions: *What supports my desires? Is it worth it for me to eat this tomato sauce when I really want to write tomorrow and need a clear brain for it? Is it worth it for me to discuss business with this writer friend who has only negative things to say all the time?*

My answer to question one—*What supports my desires?*—will give me the answer to the other questions that might arise. I want to make decisions that will help me lead the happiest, healthiest, most satisfying life possible, while being of service along the way. In order to do this, I must make choices, and those choices must be in overall alignment with my stated plans and desires.

Every relationship comes with some sort of social contract. If we're used to being around dreamers who never formulate solid plans, or unhappy people who want others to be stuck in the same mire they are, those people might get upset when we change course. We've broken the contract of dreams without action, or misery loves company, as soon as we say, "You know what? I'm not going out drinking tonight, because I want to write. Can we have breakfast on Saturday, instead?"

There might be hurt feelings from others at first. That's okay. We can reassure those friends that they are still important to us by offering alternate ways to share time. Or we might discover that the only glue holding the friendship together was our shared self-limiting behavior.

In adopting a mindset filled with possibility, we begin to make choices about our actions and where we devote most of our time and attention. In some relationships, the other person—or people—will be happy and excited to change course. "You go write!" they'll say. "I've been wanting to check out a pottery course anyway. Breakfast on Saturday sounds great."

True friends celebrate their friends.

But what about the other people? The ones who say they have your best interests at heart but are actually jealous? What about the people who want to keep everyone at their own level of smallness because they want company in their insecurity, envy, or fear?

If you want to build a successful career, I would back away from those people. Set boundaries on your energy and time.

Some people, we may need to cut out of our lives entirely. With others, it may mean limiting the sorts of interactions we have with them or choosing what we share and how.

People who are toxic to us tend to take, demand, belittle, diminish, or scorn, no matter what we do. There are people who, no matter what we say, will counter it and disagree, even when they don't know a thing about the topic. Or there are others who, when you share your shiny new cover design, will pick it apart, even though you did not ask for a critique.

This sort of behavior is a drain on our energy; it clouds our thinking and leaves us not feeling very good about ourselves or our careers. Also, these people tend to be stuck in a fixed mindset. To grow, we may need to leave them behind.

Sharing time and information with other author/publishers should feed my curiosity and help me make better choices around my career. Spending time with writers should get me excited and interested about writing and publishing and all that those entail.

Spending time with my colleagues and friends should overall leave me feeling uplifted, and not bad about myself.

Now, sometimes we feel badly about ourselves because we're trapped in comparisonitis or envy. That's on us. In these cases, it's good to ask ourselves: "Is this person really bragging, or are they celebrating their success? Is this person belittling me, or sharing what has worked for them?"

If the person is just in a different phase in

their career, maybe we can take a breath and figure out what we can learn from them. And if that feels too soon? It's okay to take some time and get our heads facing in the right direction again.

Moving away from people who are toxic to us and seeking out folks who are happy to celebrate others is a great step toward generating our own generosity and curiosity, as well as giving us more to feel thankful for!

Notice who best supports you. That's the friend who will get together with you to write... and write instead of complaining about writing. A supportive friend will listen deeply to your business plans without tearing them down. They will offer some suggestions if they have them. And they'll share their own plans with you, in turn.

To move toward a success mindset, it is our responsibility to set clear boundaries and practice upholding them. That is not on the people around us.

We are the ones who must choose.

· · ·

The Challenge

Being a creative in late capitalism is hard enough. There are those who will tell us we don't deserve to make a living, that all art should be free. I am all for the freedom of art, but also recognize that we all need to eat and pay for shelter. I give away a lot for free, because that is the sort of world I want to live in, but the more I want time to create, the more I must figure out ways to make a living.

And that's just the culture at large. What I call the overculture is currently enmeshed in not wanting to pay writers, artists, actors, or musicians at all. But the rub is: other people want to make money from the labor of those same artists. They wish to steal and exploit that labor, just as they exploit the labor of people working in factories, fields, or on warehouse floors.

As artists, we can be in solidarity with those workers all while building our own businesses.

Contradiction? Not really. As independent publishers, we run what used to be known as cottage industries. We might barter with or pay other people who have different skills than we do to help us on occasion, but most of us do not have full time workers helping us to make more cash.

But I cannot tell anyone how to behave or what choices to make regarding their own or other's labor. I can only hope that we treat each other well.

We need to find our cheerleaders and true supporters and we need to lift each other up, as well.

Depending on our upbringing, many of us have brains wired to retain harsh criticism and failure and slide over supportive words and success. When multi-award-winning author Kristine Kathryn Rusch teaches in-person writing intensives, she tells her students to write down all of her comments, good or bad. With notebooks or laptops out, people diligently comply, because her insights are so spot on. Except…Kris will often pause the person receiving notes and say, "Write that down!"

That thing that didn't get written down? Is always—without fail—positive feedback.

For too many of us, positive feedback is hard

to take in at all, let alone assimilate into our basic structure. But it is highly necessary.

The world can be harsh, and we need every glimmer of hope we can muster. This includes kind or positive reinforcement.

We've all experienced jealousy—from others or our own—and felt how much it stings. What if, instead of being jealous, we focused on our own creative ambitions and studied people who we feel are more successful than we are. What are their habits? How long did they work before getting a break? Do we even *want* their career?

Often, the answer to that final question is, "No."

That is certainly true for me. As someone in it for the long haul, I don't want to push myself as hard as some successful people do. I don't want to burn out again—I did that in my last career and recovery was intense. Also, their books are not my books!

I want to find a way to support my growth as a writer and publisher on my own terms.

And then there are the voices of our close friends or family members. Whether they are past voices we've internalized, or current, these can be the most difficult voices to ignore.

Sometimes family and friends are thrilled by our creativity and successes. Other times, they may feel threatened, jealous, or afraid for us. Family may worry that we won't be able to pay the rent. Some people who aren't building the lives *they* want may try to actively sabotage the work of their friends. I've encountered this sort of jealousy and poison from people I thought were mutual cheerleaders for our whole group.

Sometimes these voices are overt, and other times sneaky. It can take a while to wake up to the fact that someone is undermining our work. Especially if that person isn't trying to sabotage us. Maybe they think they're being supportive, but what they offer is not what we should be listening to! And sometimes? That someone is us.

So, how do we find supportive voices and stop listening to the critics? For the internalized voices, ignoring them sometimes works, at least temporarily. Musician Nancy Washer calls the inner critics her "Greek chorus" and reminds us that the chorus was often ignored by the players on the stage. So, that's one tactic.

However, we need to sense out whether ignoring the critical chorus works. Are we able to set those inner voices aside and get on with our writing? If not, we may need to actively court positive messages, using affirmations or other techniques to make our writing space more welcoming. Or we may need to see a therapist to work through this.

For the external voices, we may need to let some relationships go, or slot them into "people I see occasionally" rather than more intimate friends. And then we can reach out and begin to cultivate other, more supportive voices.

I'm not talking about sycophants and yes-people here, either. No one needs that, and surrounding ourselves with those types is as sure a way to ruin our creative careers as surrounding ourselves with people who tear us down.

I've found that truly supportive voices can be cultivated through generosity of spirit. The more supportive I am toward as wide a variety of people as I can reach, the more support I tend to attract myself. This is simpler than it may sound.

How do I do this? If I can be of help to someone who says they need it, I offer. If I can make a mutually beneficial connection between two people, I will. Along with this, I boost other people's art and projects as often as I can.

A little good will goes a long way.

The thing is, none of this is disingenuous. I'm not supporting others to get something out of it, but that does seem to be the result. I want more creativity in the world, because I firmly believe it makes the world better. So, why wouldn't I support people in this way?

And if people don't want that sort of support from me, or if what I'm offering is not right for them? I need to learn to back off and step away.

ACTION: *Are you surrounded by people who feel supportive and celebratory, or by people who are always fearful, negative, or dragging others down? What choices do you need to make around your friends, colleagues, mentors, or peers?*

8

FINDING TRUE SUPPORT

Dealing With Patterns

TO FIND TRUE SUPPORT, we may need to confront or change old patterns

I'm talking about all this as though it is easy. I know that changing patterns takes effort and time. Sometimes it takes talking things out with trusted friends or family. Sometimes it takes therapy. Other people turn to meditation, prayer, or ritual practices that help change themselves inside.

For most of us, the internal critical voices never permanently go away. That's fine. What matters is that we establish strategies to deal with the internalized critics as they arise. The other thing we can do is to recognize that we don't have to feed those voices more power. How do I starve those critical voices?

I keep writing, snapping photographs, making music, and sharing art. That's the main thing. The more I engage with creativity—mine or others—in all its forms, the less power the critical voices have.

The other thing I stopped doing was reading reviews, good or bad. Some may argue with me about this, and that's fine. But after reading reviews for a few years, I found that even the good ones were tripping me up, entering my office and my head. *"What if my next book isn't as good as that last one that people loved?"*

I don't want the pressure of other people's voices in my office when I'm writing. Not reading reviews has helped me. The support I rely on instead comes from the friends who are happy for my success and the readers who eagerly await the next story. Kind, personal notes help, too.

Another sort of support I rely upon are household members that recognize how important it is for me to keep writing and publishing. They respect my time and my efforts, help me brainstorm when I want that, and leave me to my earbuds and keyboard when I don't.

For some of us this means getting used to setting clear boundaries. "Weeknights between eight and nine are my writing time." Or "If my earbuds are in, I'm in the middle of something. Please wait until I take a break to ask me your question."

Those earbuds I'm talking about are another way I silence the critics. I already mentioned using one song on loop to get into flow. This also helps to silence random thoughts, worries, or hesitation. Every series—or sometimes individual books in the series—gets its own song. Putting that music on super low in my earbuds signals to my brain that we're writing now. It helps me bypass outside voices entirely and enter the world of my story.

That's not going to be right for everyone. But I guarantee, you have your own creativity best practices, if you allow yourself to find them.

What do you think might work for you?

People Who Believe

Find people who believe in you.

That's easier said than done, which is why it is a challenge. Finding supportive friends and colleagues may take time. Luckily, this is one thing the Internet does well, especially for writers. There are multiple groups online helping writers learn business that are surprisingly mutually supportive!

There are also groups of writers who host online writing sprints where everyone gathers on Discord, or YouTube, or Zoom and write together for twenty minutes at a time, over the course of an hour or two. There are always chat breaks in between, which are filled with support and commiseration.

But that's another challenge: we don't want too much commiseration around our creative lives.

Let me explain: Decades ago, I was in a

writing group where half the people barely wrote. Instead, there was commiseration about how hard writing was. I still see a lot of this online as well, with meme after meme about how much writers hate to write.

You know what? All that commiseration only feeds our critical voices. It's sneaky, because those voices seem as if they're supportive, but they are not! If you are in a group that constantly talks about all the reasons they're avoiding writing, and all the ways in which they suffer over their writing...run. Or, if you really like these people otherwise, you may point out this tendency and gently suggest a redirection of the group's energies and efforts to be supportive.

But when a group is entrenched in one thought-form, it can be very difficult mindset to change. Moving from a defeatist mindset to a success mindset can feel hard. And the more support there is for defeatist mindset commiseration? The more intractable the thought form becomes.

In those cases, it might be best to shift our mindset and walk away. Find a person or two who loves writing and wants nothing more than to celebrate the enjoyment of creativity, and even the enjoyment of learning how to run a business.

So, this part of the challenge is learning to distinguish between commiserating voices that only serve to keep us small, and supportive voices cheering us on.

This requires some self-examination, because early on, those commiserating voices may sound like what we need. But they aren't. They quickly become self-fulfilling traps. After all, who wants to spend time writing when it is so *hard*?

So, find people who believe in you and your work, and in their own.

Believe in yourself. And let the naysayers go their own way.

ACTION: *How often do you listen to critical voices? What are three changes you can make in your life to let more supportive voices in?*

9

BEGINNER'S MINDSET

Fresh Point of View

Zen teacher Suzuki talked about beginner's mind being one filled with many possibilities. That is important. *That* is growth mindset.

I have two thoughts regarding beginner's mindset to start us off:

Do the best you can and trust the process.

Don't put too much pressure on the writing. Who you are now isn't who you'll be five years hence. Give yourself a chance to learn and grow.

I wrote my first (complete) novel because two characters showed up and I needed to finish it. I did. Then I got a few expert readers, hired an editor, and published it.

After that? I paused, backed up, and studied as much craft as I could for a couple of years before I published again. Both publishing that first completed novel and then doing a deep dive into craft study helped me immensely.

My previous attempts at fiction writing left me with a host of unfinished, over-polished projects. Back then, I was around a lot of writers who believed in perfectionism, and that there was a *right* way to tell a story. We would give each other notes critiquing *word choice*, of all things!

Why? We were influenced by the academic study of writing, even though some of us were writing genre fiction. We hadn't yet learned that the rules of academic literary fiction are different than the rules of genre fiction. Sure, there are crossovers—literary novels rooted in story, or contemporary fiction that straddles a literary line —but mostly, literary writers are slow and more focused on ideas and language, rather than storytelling.

Not one of us in that early critique group questioned this paradigm and asked what made our favorite books so enjoyable. We lacked beginner's mind.

So, upon my return to fiction, the first thing I needed to learn was how to finish a novel at all. Then I needed to learn how to become a better storyteller. I studied genre writers much further along the path than I was to get a better handle on craft.

As a natural writer, it was good for me to learn all the things I'd skipped over when I was young because I didn't need them in order to get the rewards on offer: praise or high letter grades.

Studying craft was my focus during those first few years back, but I began to study the business of publishing as well. I made plenty of mistakes with business before retrenching yet again, the same way I did with the writing. I barreled headlong into indie publishing, and a few years in, realized I'd been studying and spending money on things that just weren't going to work for me, long *or* short term.

I hadn't asked "Why?" enough.

That's okay. Mistakes are part of how we

learn. Accepting mistakes and moving on is part of building longevity and success.

The thing about beginner's mindset is that we can pause and revisit any choice or pattern at any time.

It's so easy to get stuck in one way of doing things, especially if it worked well for a while! But the publishing landscape changes, technology shifts, trends come and go. Allowing our thinking to remain flexible and nimble will help us more in the long run than picking one thing and digging in our heels, no matter what.

A beginner's mind is filled with curiosity. I'll likely mention curiosity several times as we go along, because it is that important. One of the key phrases I use to help me invoke a curious mind is "I wonder." I began using that phrase a lot after first hearing it from author and teacher Sonia Choquette. That phrase is how she's gotten hundreds of people to deepen their intuition and psychic skills.

Sure, that may be a bit woo for some of you —sorry, I believe in magic—but that doesn't mean you can't use the power of "I wonder" for your own ends. All authors invoke wonder every time we begin writing. So why not apply that to the rest of our business, as well?

As long as we can still wonder at the world, our writing will flow. And when we apply a sense of wonder to business? Drudgery becomes play, "I have to" becomes "I get to," and the tasks we dread or fear become occasions to look at things a different way.

In calling upon beginner's mind—no matter how much breadth and depth of experience we have—we ensure that our thinking won't become brittle or bloated, and we won't ever be left behind.

If you're having trouble invoking beginner's mind with writing or the publishing business, shift gears! Take a pottery class. Join a jogging group. Learn how to garden. Tutor some kids. Practice baking. Pretty much anything new to us can become a field for learning, if we allow it to.

Back when I was traveling and teaching around the world full time, I made sure to always study something else. For quite some time, that meant I worked with a personal trainer in the gym. They pushed me to learn more about my body and mind, and challenged me long after I would have preferred to give up. I also formed a study group to read brain-cracking books adjacent to my field. Bouncing ideas off the group, and allowing myself to carefully read dense books I would otherwise avoid, broadened my thinking.

Both these physical and mental challenges pushed me past my tendencies and made me better at my work overall. They also helped set me up for career change when I needed it.

What challenges—gentle or hard—interest you right now? How can you apply that to your writing and publishing career?

ACTION: *What is one thing you can do to better embrace change and invoke beginner's mind?*

10

FIND YOUR WAY

Lane, Highway, or Winding Path

THERE IS a host of both writing and marketing advice out there and plenty of people who will tell you all the ways in which you're doing it wrong.

How to counter that? Study a lot and trust your intuition.

When I pivoted back to fiction, it seemed like the majority of independent author/publishers were talking about the Amazon algorithm and how to keep it happy. Not only were people encouraged to write and publish a book a month to feed the beast, but we were also told to "not confuse your also-boughts," aka the books people bought when they also purchased yours.

That meant people like me who seemingly write all over the map were told to use a variety of pen names. That is sound advice for some types of authors, and the kiss of death for others.

I'm in the latter camp.

So, what did I do? I said "nope." I'd built up years of goodwill with my name both by publishing nonfiction and by teaching globally. The integrity of my name was all I had. No way was I starting from scratch to keep a billionaire's machine placated.

I kept my name and kept on writing and publishing.

Guess what happened: over time, not only did my fiction overwhelm my nonfiction in searches, Amazon "also-boughts" went away completely, and the search algorithm changed. Then changed again.

Algorithms seem to change every six months to a year. Some people are good at staying ahead of this. Others of us aren't wired that way and are better off finding other ways to run our publishing businesses.

There's a similar piece of advice to the "don't pollute your also-boughts" that I repeatedly saw from certain highly successful authors, and that was, "Stay in your lane."

In other words: only write one type of book, with certain tropes, in one subgenre, in order to keep your readers coming back. Niche down and stick with it.

That advice works for some authors. It does not work for me, or for many other authors I know. We are writers first, businesspeople second. We write what we want to write when we want to write it. To a certain extent. But more on that, later.

This is where my question of "Lane or Highway" comes in. I've added a third option, which is "The Winding Path."

Some people are "Lane" writers. They want to write small town cowboy romance, or dark urban fantasy, or gutsy space opera, and their readers love it. Book after book, they love it. Lane writers often—though not always—have earlier financial success than writers like me.

Lane authors often write to market, trying to hit the correct tropes and story beats that keep readers attracted and engaged.

For some Lane writers, this works year after year, and their series expands, branches off, and multiplies. Others get bored or burn out. Or their readers get bored.

Some people are Highway writers, which is a phrase I first heard at InkersCon. This means that these authors write in many lanes, though those lanes are connected. That's likely where I fit. All of my books—even the bonkers paranormal cozy mysteries—have central themes of magic and justice. My nonfiction is no different.

While I sometimes feel I write all over the map, the reality is that I don't. What I *do* is write across genres and subgenres, with themes that please myself and my readers. This consistency of theme spills over into my newsletters, social media, and marketing. My voice is also consistent, despite some of my books being more serious than others.

Do I write to market? No. Except...I will purposefully pick some key concepts or tropes to play with in any given series. For example, why not combine three things that people love—a bookshop, a black cat, and a witch—within my own wacky, off-the-rails series? In other words, I write what I want to write, but also make sure I have some elements that will be easy to market.

And I do this consistently, feeding different series until there are enough books in them for readers to binge.

But that's just me. There are as many ways to be a Highway writer as there are writers.

Last is the Wandering Path writer. This is one that I made up because I see it all the time but have not seen it named.

Wandering Path authors write in multiple genres and subgenres but don't always have an underlying theme. There isn't huge consistency among their books. Some Wandering Path writers publish regularly and are able to build a solid, remunerative career over many years' time. But other Wandering Path writers are not consistent in their publication schedules, either, which means the business aspect of their publishing career also meanders. These writers have a much harder time building a successful business model. They're too scattershot and haphazard.

In my observation, it can take longer to find a solid readership and financial success as a Wandering Path writer in general. These writers often complain about lack of readership and nonexistent sales.

But as I mention, this does not mean other authors aren't making a go of it! Wandering Path writers can realize success. They just have to be craftier and get disciplined about publication schedules and the business side of things. They need dogged persistence, too.

This is all just a snapshot, too. Some Lane writers become Highway writers the longer their careers continue. They might write in one lane for a decade and then switch to a different lane for another decade.

Some Highway writers might wander onto a bicycle path off the freeway and stay there for a book or two, just for fun.

Some Wandering writers might fall in love with a set of characters and write four books in a row with them, forming one lane in a possible highway.

What sort of writer do you think you are, naturally?

What sort of writer would you like to be?

All of this will affect your business and your longevity. I've seen too many writers burn out and give up because they were trying to have someone else's career.

Don't let that be you.

ACTION: *What sort of writer do you think you are naturally? What sort of writer would you like to be? How can you bring these two things closer together? And why?*

Hint: Examine what most interests you and notice how that is reflected in what you write and publish.

11

SLOW AND STEADY SUCCESS

The Slow Build

I MENTIONED EARLIER that a slow build works best for me.

Early on in my fiction writing career, I paid attention to the loudest, get-rich-quick voices. It's understandable, right? Who doesn't want to be making a living right out of the gate? Who doesn't want to go from zero to six figures in a year?

In attempting to follow some of these tactics,

I went against the strategic advice of some mentors who had been in the business for decades and who talked about the long haul.

I wanted both the long haul and instant success!

Turns out the instant-success route wasn't going to work for the type of writer I was and the type of businessperson or publisher I would turn out to be. Besides which, my health tanked, leaving me physically and mentally unable to keep pace with my ambitions.

All the instant-success people were in the exclusive Kindle Unlimited program and therefore their advice about marketing—which I spent a lot of time and money studying—was not for me. To feed the exclusive KU beast is best served by publishing at least one book a month and being a Lane writer.

Turns out I have a chronic illness and am a Highway writer. I spent six months in KU with one series and had some modest success before that petered out and I withdrew my books again. I needed to re-strategize.

What I really needed was to learn what I call the slow build.

So, what did I do? I took three steps back, and focused on writing and craft, studying business all the while.

That was most certainly the right choice. It's also the right choice for most writers who want to build a professional career.

I'll likely repeat this several times in these pages, but the most common answer newer writers get to their questions about how to successfully market a book is *"Write the next book."*

This is not the answer most newer writers want to hear, but it is the correct answer, at least early on. If we want to be successful in reaching readers and making a living, the best thing to sell a book is the next five books. This can feel like harsh advice at first, but that doesn't negate its truth.

Writing the next book gives us practice. Writing the next book buys us time. Writing the next book increases our chances of discoverability, and discoverability is the most important tool in the marketing kit.

We'll talk more about marketing later.

What else is involved in the slow build? Getting to know what we enjoy writing and what our readers respond to. That doesn't mean reading reviews and tailoring our writing toward that. We get to know what our readers respond to by seeing what sells over time.

After writing two serious urban fantasy series and in the midst of writing an epic, action-adventure fantasy romance trilogy, I sustained my brain injury. Once I was well enough to write again, my brain still needed a break. Tracking multiple points of view in my fantasy trilogy was not going to work. Instead, I embarked upon writing a bonkers, paranormal cozy mystery series that is now my biggest seller.

Go figure.

If I hadn't been open to what came next, I would never have known the joys of introducing readers to a lively cast of characters in a truly strange seaside town. And I wouldn't be making the income from that series, either.

And yes, dear reader, I finished the fantasy trilogy as well. It just took a bit more time.

Building a Business

. . .

Common wisdom tells us that it takes two to three years for a new business to turn a profit. That's *any* profit. It takes seven to ten years of diligent work for a new business to become successful. If the business survives.

What helps a business survive? Many factors, of course. But the most important thing is this: the business founder did not give up.

Most of us want a quick fix and overnight success. Why wouldn't we? It's okay to want that. However, there's an old joke that says overnight success takes ten years. Hmmm...

I've also seen too many authors with early success peter out and stop. Why? I think their critical voice took over and throttled their creativity. It's hard to create when we think we need to live up to outside expectations.

As I write this, there are birds outside singing. That makes me smile. To me, they are making music. What are they actually doing? They're talking to each other. Or maybe they're happy and sounding off to the world. What they aren't doing is saying: "Is today's song as good as yesterday's song? Will my friends the next tree over like my song? What if they don't like it? Should I quit singing?"

The birds just practice singing. Writers just practice writing. It's all just communication.

As I've already said, the reason some of those early-success authors stop is because of burn out. They get on a hamster wheel of unsustainable production, try to meet reader expectations, and eventually they get tired, or their creative voice gets cranky at the forced march.

This isn't about writing fast versus writing slow, either (see Tracy Cooper-Posey's book, *The Productive Indie Fiction Writer*, on that argument). It's about attempting to force creativity into a form or rhythm that isn't *our* form or rhythm.

The creative voice loves to frolic, experiment, and play. When we get caught up in comparing ourselves to other writers and the success of their communication, our song eventually dries up.

Comparison can be useful when we use it for inspiration. I like studying what other artists and writers are doing. Sometimes there are ways they connect with their work or with their readers/audience that intrigue me. Is that something that I might experiment with? When? Is there something here I can study and perhaps enact within the next month? Six months? Or is this a thing I want to hold in reserve and look at again a year from now?

Or…I might decide it likely isn't for me, and me wishing it would be is really just a fear of missing out. Fear of missing the Next Big Thing.

Let's use TikTok as an example. There was a whole lot of FOMO happening there for a while, when BookTok was seemingly making authors into overnight successes. A lot of authors flocked to the social platform, trying to catch some of the faery dust.

I gave it a stab. Inconsistently and briefly. Trouble is, TikTok is exactly the sort of platform that my brain loathes. Constant movement, things leaping about, noise, flashing…ugh. That's *my* experience of the platform, with no offense to anyone who loves it. I do find occasional entertainment at people's TikTok videos, they're often clever, and I admire that.

But as a platform, and for me? Nope. If I dislike using it that much, why would I think my videos would be things that other people connect with?

So, I dropped my fear of missing out, dropped my comparison to these authors who were blowing up on TikTok, and went back to what works for me: the slow, steady, build.

Why Slow?

I COMBAT comparisonitis and the fear of missing out with the slow build. The slow build requires some getting used to, and the ability to try things and discard them, while trying and keeping other techniques. In other words, the slow build relies upon experimentation and finding our own patterns.

The opposite of a singular lottery win or lightning strike or get-rich-quick scheme, the slow build is one way to grow a sustainable business from the art we put out into the world.

I firmly believe we can create and build a business in a way that brings us joy.

This takes time, and yes, it takes a shift in mindset.

The hustle mindset tells us that we're failures if we don't make two hundred grand overnight. The hustle mindset tells us that we're failures if we're not always grinding and burning the candle at both ends.

It's funny, because when people talk about "fixed mindset" and "growth mindset," some of us think that growth mindset is one of hustle and grind. But in my experience, the hustle and grind mindset can be just as fixed, if not more, as a mindset that tells us we'll never make it, no matter how hard we try.

What I'm talking about here is shifting our mindset from one that is limiting to a mindset filled with possibility. That is where growth happens.

So, just as I mentioned the defeatist and success mindsets, I'll introduce their companions: the limiting mindset and the possibility mindset.

A limiting mindset insists on only one thing. A possibility mindset is curious and likes to explore different avenues toward success.

A limiting mindset tells us either that things

will never really change, or that it will take constant, heroic effort on our parts, or a major piece of random luck.

A possibility mindset tells us that there's a lot we don't know, but we can practice and learn.

Now, for some people, the possibility mindset opens opportunity very quickly. If that's you, go for it! I've certainly been that person in the past. Sometimes this worked well for me, and other times it was to my detriment because I ended up too far ahead of the curve, which can be as difficult on success as being too far behind.

But, despite my ambitions, I am not a hustle and grind person when it comes to my writing and publishing business.

Every time I tried to hustle and get ahead quickly, things did not work. At all. Part of that was the struggle I was engaged with in the early days of my return to writing fiction. After years of spotty treatment because of a lack of diagnosis, my chronic illness was acute, and I'd not yet learned how to stabilize the symptoms. Plus, I quit one career, moved states, bought a house, dealt with my mother's death process...and then sustained a brain injury.

There was no way hustle culture was going to serve me during such a cascade of circumstances.

So, what did serve me? Consistently showing up for my writing. Adjusting my publishing schedule to be more manageable. Figuring out what sorts of marketing actually work for me.

The main thing that served me, though, was not giving up.

That's right: I built my publishing business during the eight most challenging years of my adult life. And I'm thriving now, even with my minor disabilities.

A‍ction: *Take a good look at your ambitions. How long do you think you can sustain your writing and publishing schedule in order to support those ambitions? What changes can you put in place to help your longevity?*

12

FINANCIAL MINDSET

What is the Platform for Your Financial Dreams?

CREATING a platform for our financial dreams might require a shift toward possibility and success mindset for many of us. It is easy to feel discouraged when starting—or maintaining—a creative business. There is so much to learn! Discoverability is hard!

The first thing I suggest all would be midlist indie authors do is to set some financial milestones. Do you want to pay for editing? Do you want to pay for editing and your monthly phone bill? Do you want to level up from there and bring in $1000 a month? $5000? $10,000?

Set a realistic goal first. Jumping from operating at a loss to $5000 a month is not likely. A healthy mindset is to allow ourselves to be happy with our gains, while stair-stepping our way to larger gains—if that is what we want. And of course, study your country's tax codes while you're at it.

Another key financial mindset is to double down on enjoying writing itself. When our mindset tips into being all about the money, the writing will slowly begin to suffer and feel like a chore. That's not a great way to make a living. First off, your mind and heart and body will notice. Second, your readers will notice, too.

In assessing business and financial goals, we need to ask: What is important to me? Is it the latest model car or computer? Or is it greater financial flexibility that allows me time to write?

We all have different responsibilities and are in different phases of our lives, so every person's relationship to finances and expenses will be different. Financial teacher Ramit Sethi asks people what their rich life is. For me, my rich life has always included prioritizing time for creativity. This means my career choices have been...odd but satisfying. They've also been terrific fodder for my writing!

Since you are reading this book, I will assume you want to make more money with your writing. This requires making choices. How much money will you invest in next year's holiday versus how much money will you invest into your writing business?

I know writers who are terrified to spend any money on their writing business because they aren't yet making any money. I know other writers who pour thousands into their writing career, making each book so expensive to produce that it slows down their production time and then begins to slow down their writing.

Both of these types of writers need a mindset shift. The first writers need to comprehend that they are indeed running a business and that businesses have overhead. Both sets of writers must get crafty with targeting spending wisely. They might figure out how to do some things themselves. Maybe they need to study cashflow. I can recommend Michael Warren Lucas's book *Cashflow for Creators*.

Can we apply our creativity to our business? Of course! Getting creative is necessary, plus, it makes business more fun.

So, when building a financial platform, here's what I suggest: set some targets. These can be loose or firm.

Brainstorm as many ways to make money from writing and publishing as you can. This list will expand the more you study things like copyright and licensing. Then look at that list and choose the three items that feel most interesting to you.

Next, set yourself a timeline to learn and implement the first of those ways to make money. I suggest three to six months.

And finally, keep invoking curiosity and patience.

ACTION: *What is your current financial goal regarding writing and publishing? What is one action you can take to help yourself reach that goal?*

. . .

SLASHING Personal Expenses

ONE WAY TO achieve our financial goals more quickly is to cut our expenses.

Slashing expenses also requires a mindset and priorities shift.

One thing I did when transitioning out of my previous career and focusing on fiction was to slash my personal expenses. I knew I would need some wiggle room during the transition while I figured things out.

I instigated a massive cut in expenses by convincing my family that moving from the Berkeley/Oakland border in California to Portland, Oregon, was the right thing to do. This cut our expenses by half.

It was a good thing we made the move, because my undiagnosed health issues finally caught up with me right after that. If I'd still had a crushing SF Bay Area mortgage and other higher life expenses (have you ever eaten out in San Francisco?), I would have been in big trouble and unable to meet those bills.

As it was, slashing expenses gave me a cushion so I could work at my business part time when I could barely leave the couch. I established writing and publishing rhythms while figuring out how to get my health back on a more even keel.

My situation was extreme. Yours doesn't have to be.

But I'll give you another example: when I was a young, anarchist punk, I took a job on the Pacific Stock Options Exchange to learn about economics while getting paid. I have a lot of stories from that time, let me tell you! But one thing I'll never forget is working there during the big crash of 1987. All these people who had bought mansions and boats while riding high were in a sudden panic. They were going to lose everything.

Me? I had been raised working class/working poor and knew how to live on almost nothing. I knew then that no matter what happened, I was adaptable and would be fine.

How quickly could you adapt if your income suddenly dropped? Or are you maxed out on car payments, high rent, credit card debt, a million kid's activities, a shoe addiction, tuition, elder care, or eating out?

I'm mentioning this here because adaptability is a big part of the indie midlist author mindset. As authors, our income will always fluctuate. Establishing multiple streams of income within and around the writing sphere helps to even out these dips—things like subscriptions can offer a steady monthly income over time, for example—but if we are trained to panic with each fluctuation, this career is likely going to be more stressful than we can manage.

Finance teacher Ramit Sethi says that our fixed costs should remain between 50% and 60% of our net income. Net income is what the average worker takes home after taxes, and does not include things like retirement contributions, which are a separate category.

So, let's do a little experiment: write down all your fixed expenses.

- rent or mortgage
- car payment
- phone, Internet, all other utilities
- groceries

- tuition or other activity payments
- gym fees
- credit card debt or student loan payments…

Your list is likely longer or slightly different, but you get the idea. Fixed costs are anything you pay out regularly, every month. That debt payment only includes *carried* debt and does not include using a credit card with a balance that you pay off every month.

Once you tally up all your fixed expenses, what's the percentage of your take-home income they consume? That's the first step at assessing your personal finances.

Next: is it possible to cut any of your fixed expenses, and get your percentage down to 50% of net or under?

For example, before Covid hit, my family had grown profligate with our grocery spending. Once prices began to rise, I took things in hand and started cutting that bill. We purchased a chest freezer to buy more in bulk and now "shop the freezer" for dinner. Even as grocery prices continue to rise, we've kept that expense down to far below what it was pre-pandemic times.

How had the grocery bill risen so high in the first place? We are privileged enough that just weren't paying attention. Once I started taking physical receipts and tallying total grocery expenditure at month's end, it became easier to lower the cost and keep it down.

The lower your fixed expenses are, the easier it will be to transition into writing full time if that's your goal.

Business Expenses

NOW LIST YOUR BUSINESS EXPENSES. When you're first starting out, you'll have different expenses than after you've been at it for a while. The time you spend on business will also change.

Early on, focus should be on writing and studying the industry. After you have a few books out, you can add in more business tasks and time.

Once you enter the indie author world, you

may also be bombarded by a dozen different courses guaranteed to make you rich! Learn cost per click ads! Take my course on subscriptions or direct sales!

I took some of those expensive classes way too early in my indie author career when frankly, it was too soon for them to help me. Why? I didn't know the lay of the land yet. Other than a vague dream, I didn't know what sort of author career I wanted. I didn't know what to look out for, either so couldn't accurately assess which course might be of most use.

The classes that helped me the most were all on improving my craft.

Now that I'm better established, I know what angles of business to study and can assess which books or courses—if any—will be of help.

Luckily, the indie author world is filled with people who are happy to help each other. All that takes is joining some Discord, Circle, or Facebook groups, reading author blogs, listening to podcasts, reading books, and studying as much as you can. This helps you learn what questions to even ask.

. . .

HERE ARE some possible business expenses:

- Copyediting or proofreading (some people use beta readers for the first rounds of this. I don't want that much input into my creative process. I have one first reader to tell me if things don't make sense, then hire a combo copy and line editor to catch typos and continuity mistakes. One of my loyal readers then does another pass after that to find any typos the editor missed. Because that always happens).
- Book cover design.
- Cover design software (if you're doing covers yourself, like I do).
- Interior formatting software (like Atticus, Vellum, or InDesign. You can also do this for free at first by uploading a PDF to Draft2Digital.)

- Bookfunnel or StoryOrigin (for ebook delivery and author-run promotions).
- Website hosting.
- Tax-accounting software and/or human.
- Newsletter provider (most are free up to a certain number of subscribers, or you can use a monetizable newsletter platform, which I switched to when I got tired of paying for a fancy newsletter provider. I now make steady money from that, as well).

NOTE THAT, other than Bookfunnel, which has multiple uses, I did not mention marketing expenses! Again, until you have a few books out, all your marketing efforts should be no cost other than some time spent sending out a newsletter or posting on social media.

Some people will tell you to spend thousands of dollars on publishing each book. In reality, you should be able to publish a book for very little. Either buy a premade cover or learn to design them yourself. Scouring the daily Bookbub emails or scrolling through covers on retailers are great ways to study covers in your genre!

Comb through your book on Word—or a program like ProWritingAid—looking for red underlines that might indicate a typo. Then ask a trusted friend to read it and mark any mistakes they see. Hire an editor from an author group, or someplace like Fiverr. Test them out until you find one that respects your author voice. Remember, grammar and punctuation are part of your author voice. Fiction does not need to be written with correct grammar!

Some people will encourage you to hire a developmental editor. That's its own mindset, and is up to you, but I generally recommend against it. Developmental editors are very expensive and will tell you how to "fix" your story. Some authors use this process to study craft, which is great. It just doesn't work for me.

I'd rather read a craft book or take a class. Why? Much of the time, developmental editors find insecure new writers who don't believe in their work yet. Unless you are very strong in yourself and know how to reject as well as accept feedback, I think this is overall detrimental to the natural process of finding your own author voice. If you trust yourself, have the money, and want a fresh perspective, a developmental editor might be of help. In that case, I would find one who is also a writer, because they'll have a deeper understanding of craft than someone who has never written a book in their life.

But the overall best fix for a story? Finish it and write the next one. Study your favorite authors. Throw the proverbial one hundred clay pots and get better as you go. No book is perfect, and that's part of their charm. We all learn as we go, and there is nothing wrong with that.

As your book catalog, income, and business grow, you can choose to add more expenses, but be judicious about it. I paid to set up a C corporation once my publishing income grew large enough to pay taxes on it. That's also when I hired a tax accountant.

I still weigh what continuing education is worthwhile to pay for and what I can study on my own.

I hired a lawyer to go over my three old traditional contracts to see what, if anything, might be possible to do with the ideas inside and the books themselves. This was worth the one-time cost because it helped me plot out a ten-year nonfiction plan and get the rights back to a book I thought was lost to me forever.

Your business is different than mine and anybody else's, but there is a lot we can learn from each other. What that takes is self-knowledge and discernment. Don't let fear or hype rule your actions. Use both your mind and your intuition as guides. What makes the most sense for your career right now?

And always, the best marketing you can do is to write and publish another book. The main cost of that is time.

ACTION: *Make a list of your basic recurring expenses, including subscriptions, groceries, car payment, rent, phone bill, etc. What percentage of your take home pay is that? Are there any expenses you can cut back on? What are you willing and able to invest in your business?*

13

INCOME STREAM MINDSET

Building Multiple Streams

MY PATH toward midlist indie success has been achieved by building multiple income streams, and most of them are direct-to-reader.

If you are a writer with fewer than five books out, don't scatter yourself too much, too fast. Building your catalog is your primary task. If you enjoy steady reader engagement, you might try out something like Royal Road or Ream. If that's not you, you might experiment with something like Kickstarter, allowing it to build as you go. Even if these activities "only" net enough profit to pay for editing, covers, or ISBNs, I would consider that a success. Plus, you'll be learning how to leverage different business strategies and gaining familiarity with how these platforms work. In other words, you'll be getting paid to learn.

Regardless of how many books are in your catalog, building multiple income streams requires a measure of curiosity, the spirit of experiment, and motivation. I've seen successful authors consider their Kickstarter campaigns a failure, despite the fact that they funded! Perhaps the platform really did not work for them, or perhaps they gave up too soon. That's only for them to say. But I always want to invoke curiosity and the spirit of testing. As I used to tell my students: try this out for six months to a year before deciding it doesn't work for you.

So, what about motivation? Motivation, for me, is internal. I'm a self-starter, and am good at setting goals and making commitments. Multiple streams of income require both, but making several small goals and commitments feels far less onerous to me than making one large, steady business or writing commitment.

Without that flexibility, I would not be nearly as successful, and without internal motivation, I would likely just be spinning my wheels.

But what about people who need external motivation? If that's you, you might corral an accountability buddy or two, join online public writing or business-task sprints like the kind hosted by Sarra Cannon's Heart Breathings crew, or Writers With Wings, or several others. Ask a couple of writer friends if they want to study marketing and discuss your findings once a month. Set a publication schedule and stick with it. Join a challenge....

You can find a way to make this business work in a way that suits you. There's no one true way, regardless of what anyone says.

ACTION: *Know your own tendencies. If you are an externally motivated person, what do you think would help the most? If you are an internally motivated person, what are you most excited to try?*

· · ·

My Current Income Streams

My current income streams are the following, in no particular order:

- Patreon
- Kickstarter
- A Monetized Newsletter
- Direct Website Sales
- Direct Events Sales
- All Retailer Platforms
- Libraries
- Ebooks
- Print
- Special Editions
- Exclusive Omnibus Editions
- Book-Related Merchandise
- Short Story Sales to Magazines or Anthologies
- Foreign Rights Licensing

OTHER AUTHORS ADD IN TRANSLATION, audio, radio plays, graphic novels, film options...you get the picture.

I could also show you the many trickles that form each stream above. Every single book and short story have their own trickles that form an income stream.

I could add in the online classes I ran two or three times a year until recently—pre-recorded evergreen material which was almost truly passive income—and the handful of one-on-one coaching clients I still have. Those activities link directly to my nonfiction books—both my traditional and now indie titles—so could be considered writing-related income.

All of these streams add up to high five figures in revenue per year and climbing. Long-term thinking, remember? This means that, despite my autoimmune disorder, brain injury aftermath, and knowing that some days I only have the brain or energy to work a couple of hours, I can support myself and grow my business in a sustainable manner.

And since I run my business as a *business*, most of that revenue stays put. What do I mean by that? Well, I am not a tax advisor, accountant, or lawyer, so this is just what I've done, using some advice from well-established writers and indie publishers: after years of running a sole proprietorship, I formed a C corporation, which, in many other countries is just a standard corporation.

Why? I did this because I was making enough profit to pay taxes on my writing business income and to help simplify my business life. I didn't want a "pass through" like an S corp or LLC because I wanted a clear wall between my personal money and business money. I did this with an eye toward growth.

Again, I am not an expert on tax law and you'll need to make your own decisions around this. After doing research, other authors often choose a different corporate structure. Do what seems best for your business. If you're starting out, a DBA (Doing Business As) or its equivalent in your country is a good choice.

Running a C corporation in the US means that all my business expenses are pre-tax instead of post-tax. That's right, all the books I buy for entertainment and study are purchased on a corporate card as legitimate business expenses. The same with hotels and flights for business travel. No more trying to figure out write-off percentages.

My corporation also pays my salary, so I know exactly how much personal money I have coming in every month. And since I slashed my expenses when I pivoted from my other career? I don't even need that much to live on, which increases my ability to be nimble and take some business risks.

I'm grateful for my success, and know I have a good foundation—and the right attitude—to weather any ups and downs that may come.

You'll need to do your own research and make your own decisions. Cultivate a clear mind and patience. It's okay to take your time.

ACTION: *How many income streams do you currently have, including a day job? What is one income stream you can work on adding over the next three months?*

. . .

Subscriptions Mindset

The first building blocks of my author-publisher success came, not from book sales on retailers, but from subscriptions. Subscriptions still form the foundation of my author business. Other authors might have the opposite experience. But even some of those authors have shifted toward things like direct sales or subscriptions as the publishing landscape continues to evolve.

Getting away from the mindset that if we aren't making bank from retailer book sales right away, we aren't successful, is the first change many of us need to make. I know I did.

I believe that it is time to shift our vision of success. Success has layers and levels. Recognizing this helps us foster a healthy attitude. If we latch onto one thing as the pinnacle of success, we'll either feel crushed if we don't reach it, or bored and disappointed once we do reach that elusive thing.

It is far more sustainable to set several small success goals and see what happens on the way.

For me, the first layer of success is writing and publishing books. Not many people do that, despite insisting they want to! The second layer of success is reaching readers and fans. It doesn't matter how I get there. The third layer of success is making a living.

By using subscriptions—Patreon and a beehiiv newsletter for me—I have established a steady, consistent base for the rest of my income to grow upon. Book sales rise and fall, but most people, once signed up for a subscription service, have a set and go attitude. It's rare to revisit a subscription more than once a year, if that. Most of us happily pay, month after month, year after year, until and unless we have a large change in our finances, or the subscription service does something egregious that makes us pay attention and cancel.

How many subscriptions do you pay for right now? What are your expectations around those services, be they television, films, podcasts, music, or books?

I support several people on Patreon and have for years. A couple of those subscriptions are ones I pay closer attention to, and "get my money's worth" from. But most often, I don't even engage with the subscription, I just want those people to be doing their work in the world with the support of my five dollars a month.

A lot of people are that way. Others are the type of fans who love nothing more than engaging with their favorite authors.

I get sporadic engagement from my Patreon supporters and much more regular engagement from my newsletter readers because that subscription is more of a conversation than a random weekly offering, if that makes sense.

What sort of writer are you? What sort of public presence do you want? How might you connect with people via subscriptions?

This doesn't have to be a big numbers game, either. That's a mindset shift many people need to get beyond. It doesn't matter whether your newsletter has five subscribers or five thousand. What matters is the quality of connection. The same is true of any subscription model, whether it is free or paid.

Author Kristine Kathryn Rusch reminds us that we build our audience one reader at a time, and for me, that is what subscriptions and other forms of crowdfunding do.

Once we free ourselves of the pressure to gain thousands of sign-ups or hundreds of dollars, we can enjoy the journey, experiment, and figure out what works best for ourselves and our readers.

I've changed my Patreon several times over the almost decade I've been on that platform. My interests have changed, as has the focus of my work. My patrons seem happy to roll with whatever I decide works for me. I lose and gain folks, of course, but overall, my subscriptions are quite stable, and lately have been increasing again. And despite offering my newsletter for free, a steady percentage of readers want to pay me for it because they appreciate my weekly musings in their inbox, or my daily social media posts.

The funny thing is, you can call all of it a form of content marketing. I just call it connection. I'm grateful for that connection, and for the money, too.

There is no one way to approach subscriptions. Nothing makes me more tense about my subscription models than comparing myself to other writers and how they run their subscriptions. I'll start thinking, "My writing career is so weird, if I only ever wrote cozy mysteries, it would be so much easier to reach people."

But my readers love my work *because* I'm weird! A colleague once said that no matter what subgenre I'm writing in, it's all clearly me, and clearly designed to reach my readers. Another colleague calls this trait my "Thornocity."

See, it's hard to recognize our own authorial voice. Apparently, mine is quite consistent, despite my sometimes feeling as if I'm all over the map.

The way multi-six-figure author Emilia Rose runs her subscriptions is never going to work for me. Does that mean I'll never make as much money as she does? Probably. But I'm okay with that, because trying to shoehorn myself into her career is only going to alienate my readers and make me miserable.

I must find my own success, just as you have to find yours.

A successful mindset regarding subscriptions might look like this: "I enjoy reaching readers and will create ways to connect that are easy, simple, and satisfying."

ACTION: *Have you researched subscription models? Are you already running subscriptions? Take some time and figure out what attracts and what scares you about connecting with readers via subscriptions.*

Next: What mindset shift will free you up to have as much success as possible with subscriptions? Or are subscriptions not right for you in this moment in your career?

There aren't any wrong answers here, just the ability to learn, explore, and make a decision about what direction you want to go.

14

RETURNING TO FOCUS

Some Thoughts on Focus

IT IS easy to feel overwhelmed, but that is a mindset, too. How do we combat overwhelm and fractured attention?

Focus on one strategy at a time, and don't give up.

There are author/publishers who consistently work twelve-hour days. I'm not one of them. With my health and my brain issues, I cannot be. I tend to work seven days a week, sometimes all day, but other days? I feel as if I do not work at all, putting in an hour, or maybe two. And sometimes I take the entire day off as a reset.

So, how have a become a successful midlist author? Focus, tenacity, and a long-term view.

Rather than running myself ragged trying to do all the things, I pick one or two things at a time, get those systems in place—or jettison what did not work for me—and then add something else. This is all part of how my mindset links up with my actions.

I know I will post to social media daily. I know I will post to Patreon and send out a newsletter weekly. I have Kickstarter campaigns to work on. Books to write. But I didn't always. I began with writing and social media, then added publishing and Patreon. Only once those felt solid did I add still more new things. The best thing I did three years ago was shifting my sporadic newsletter to one with a weekly cadence. I get more organic growth that way.

The other activity I spend time on is industry research and study. I do this over breakfast or lunch or listening to podcasts on walks. On days when my brain is tired and not able to do much tricky or generative work very well, that study is the only work activity I will do. Reading novels becomes my research on my worst days.

I also do my best to notice what works for me, and what does not.

There are writers building out direct sales stores—which is a great overall tactic, by the way—who barely write and publish. These people *might* be letting their dreams get in the way of building a sustainable reality, and we'll talk more about dreams in another mindset section. But these writers might also be taking a year or so to set a long-term plan in place, while preparing for slow growth. I can't know from the outside.

I can only hope those writers have a conscious strategy instead of jumping on a current "you must do this to succeed" bandwagon.

What would *I* do were I one of these writers? I would build out my web store, for sure. And as a person with a solid catalog, I have. But what if I did not have a solid catalog yet? I might acknowledge that I was building my shop in order to have a system in place for the future, reminding myself that is an important part of the process.

When I know *why* I'm doing something, I have better context for *how* it relates to my business long-term.

"Everyone is doing it," is not a good *why*, because someone else's strategy may have very little relationship to the *how* of our own businesses.

But mostly, if I was a person who was barely writing or publishing? I would focus on the *writing* for a set period of time. I'd put my butt in the chair or my feet on the treadmill and write and publish some more. That's the basis of the slow build for most of us.

To build a long-term career, we need writing, publishing, marketing, and business to all be in play. Few people can balance all four of these equally, at all times. Most of us focus on the writing and publishing, and work in marketing and business around that. Why? Writing and publishing is the bedrock of our author business. Period.

But in reality, all four legs of the chair will gain prominence during different phases of our careers. An author with a sixty-book catalog is in a very different position than an author who has published five books. The former can focus more on business and marketing, while the latter should be more focused on writing and publishing.

The writer with two hundred books published or more? Their career choices will be different, still. Some of those writers expand their publishing business, branching out into merchandising, publishing other authors, or any number of strategies that just don't make sense to those of us who are not there yet, or don't want to be.

What the rest of us can do is look at these prolific author's business practices and wonder *why* they are making the choices they make. I guarantee that their business includes a solid *how* that corresponds with that *why*.

And remember, business changes. Even those writers with massive catalogs need to pivot sometimes in order to keep their business healthy, relevant, and moving with the times.

ACTION: *Take a good look at where you are in your career. How many books have you published? How many series do you have in circulation? What mar-*

kets are you currently tapping? What is your proposed writing and publishing schedule for the next year? The next five years?

Write all of those numbers down, then ask yourself: What is the best next step to support both my business why *and* how?

15

TACKLING RESISTANCE

What Are You Avoiding?

CREATIVITY REQUIRES relationship with the world around us. We can create in a vacuum for only so long, until the well runs dry.

We all need space and time to refill the well. This looks slightly different for each of us. It might be going for a walk outside, or listening to music, or reading a favorite author, watching a movie, dipping our toes in the ocean, or taking a nap.

But to paraphrase indie author Tracy Cooper-Posey, sometimes relaxation becomes avoidance. Sure, we need a break, but when we end up with excuse after excuse getting in the way of our writing and attending to our business? We need to set an alarm to give ourselves a wakeup call.

Newton's Laws of Motion tell us: a body in motion stays in motion, and a body at rest stays at rest.

In other words, we are all affected by inertia. If we're in motion, writing on a regular schedule, publishing on a regular schedule, marketing on a regular schedule…inertia takes over and makes all the above much easier. It's what pilots call "ground effect," a term I first heard from romantic thriller author M. L. Buchman. A plane in motion just coasts along, barely needing any effort to stay aloft.

But when that same plane comes to a full stop? Starting again takes a lot more energy and effort. And when that plane has been stopped for a long time? Even more effort is required because engine parts may need cleaning or de-rusting. Fuel lines may need to be cleared...you get the picture.

Our creative selves can become rusty, as well. A working writer engages in small, regular acts of maintenance. This doesn't have to mean daily writing for all of us, though that helps many of us. All I'm saying is: the less we write, the more difficult writing becomes. A non-working writer usually needs a lot more work and effort to get back into the flow.

If we add rest and well-filling into our daily lives —along with our writing and business practices— we tend toward ground effect. Support of our creativity means our creativity can, in turn, support us. Life, writing, and yes, even business, all become easier to handle. We cultivate a greater sense of ease and joy in the process, even when times feel tough.

I see so many writers who go through life challenges and simply stop engaging with their creativity. They take some needed time off to deal with their own health, or a family crisis, and then...kinda sorta never come back.

They end up reverting to amateur status. And not the sort of amateur who engages with their craft regularly and with love and interest. That's a fantastic kind of amateur to be. I'm that sort of amateur with photography, and I love it.

The reversion I'm talking about show up in the following patterns: Thinking we'll wait to write until we feel inspired. Or we won't write until our energy and attention levels are perfect, and our crowded schedule clears itself. We'll wait until the Muse strikes....

These stalled-out people don't really want to be professional writers, but they've also not admitted to giving up on the dream of being a professional. They haven't embraced amateur status. Will they ever recommit? Perhaps. I certainly did. But I had to stop saying I wanted it, first. And then, when I *did* decide I wanted it, I had to commit to coming back.

After years of being an on-again, off-again journalist and poet, and laboring over one short story a year all while making stabs at writing novels that I never finished, I gave up fiction entirely, recognizing that being a novelist was a fantasy and not a true desire.

I needed to do some other things with my life

for a decade, including traditionally publishing those three nonfiction books on spiritual practice and traveling the world, teaching. Then, when I was ready, I fully committed to fiction and later, by putting nonfiction back into the mix, to writing as a whole. And that's where I am now.

So, there is nothing wrong with any of these phases we might find ourselves in. What I'm asking us all to do is to sense more clearly what we really want and bring our words and actions closer together.

Don't say you want to be a professional writer when you're doing next to nothing to make the dream come true. Write! Have fun! Take the pressure off your creativity and see what happens next. That is likely the best gift a stuck writer can give themselves.

Then....if you want to make a living as a writer, at a certain point you must commit. The first commitment is to write as much as you can and study your craft. The second commitment is to learn business and figure out what sort of business you want to run.

This book talks about what has worked for

me, and I hope it will give you inspiration to chart your own course.

What Resistance Tells Us

Sometimes bumping up against resistance is a sign we're trying to do things too quickly, or we're headed the wrong direction. Other times, it's a sign we're exhausted and need some deep rest or a reset.

But most of the time, I find that resistance means I'm over-complicating things. Just as in writing, we can take Dean Wesley Smith's advice and "write the next sentence" to break our resistance, we can do the same with business.

When I resist taking on a vital business task, I take a breath and say, "Just do one thing." Or other times the message is, "Just try."

Action: *Write down one thing you're willing to commit to, today, regarding your writing and publishing career.*

16

HOW ABOUT READERS?

Fostering Connection

MUCH AS SOME of us would like to write and publish in complete isolation, that simply is not practical. Readers must be able to find us, and that means we have to find ways to reach them. I used to moan that I wished I could just throw money at the problem but found that did not work for me. Paid advertisements were useless in my early days of publishing novels.

Why? I was using methods championed by

writers who had larger catalogs and completely different styles and careers than I did. These days, I've drilled down on what paid opportunities do work for my career, and happily spend a hundred or more dollars a month on that. Other people spend thousands. That works for them. That was likely never going to work for me.

So, I'll ask: What is your preferred way to connect with readers, supporters, or fans? Do you know?

It's hard to know when starting from scratch. One useful tactic is to study how your favorite writers in your favorite genres connect. Might any of those methods work for you?

If you are in an exclusive ecosystem like Kindle Unlimited, paid cost per click ads might be your jam. But there are other ways to connect, too.

Lindsey Buroker makes social media posts about dragons. Gail Carriger posts fancy teacups. Other authors have a fan-favorite character "write" their newsletter.

A lot of us also connect with readers via free first in series strategies coupled with paid newsletters such as Bookbub, Freebooksy, and all the rest. I use that method to great effect. My Bookbub months are currently the only time my ad spend goes over $150. As my website store grows, that figure will change as I experiment with adding a few cost per click ads back into my mix, to funnel readers to my personal webstore. I plan to experiment with this for a year to see how it goes!

But mostly, for me, what I consider is how to build a long-term relationship with readers, instead of figuring out how to simply sell the next book. I need both! My tendency is to not want to advertise, and just to connect, but the reality is, the books I write are a major part of what I want to communicate to readers! I don't just want them to read three hundred words about my week. I want them to fall in love with my characters and my worlds. I want my stories to make them think or laugh.

I've figured out what works for me, for now. I'm sure that will change over time, as well. But my overall aim is always clear: I want to change the world through words.

To build a sustainable career, we need to not only figure out what we most love to write, we need to figure out what sort of marketing we like. And if that means starting by figuring out what sort of marketing least makes us want to stab ourselves with a fork? So be it.

The thing is, we have to try. And that means…actually trying. Experimenting. Practicing. Testing something out for six months to a year and then assessing both the results and how we feel about the forms of marketing we've chosen.

Long term, remember? Testing for a year is nothing in the larger scheme of an author-publisher career. Our systems don't need to work right out of the gate. We get to test and practice as we go.

Speaking of…by figuring out what works for us and testing, I am in no way saying that we can't whine, stamp our feet, and say, "I hate marketing (or business)." If you don't want to learn business or marketing, that is totally fine! You can write and put out books when you want to, have a lovely Wandering Path career or hobby, and make some coffee money while you're at it.

There is nothing wrong with that.

I repeat: There is nothing wrong with that.

Frankly, I wish more people would take the win of writing and publishing and selling any copies at all and deciding that's what they enjoy! Figuring out that we don't really want to run a business is as much a victory as figuring out how to run a business.

I have friends who write and publish and study, preparing to make some additional income after they retire from their current day job or career. That's a terrific plan! They're building up a catalog of books, learning how to gain a handful of new readers every year, making a small trickle of money, and prepping for the day when they'll have more time to devote to publishing. Solid.

There are other writers I know who thoroughly enjoy writing fan fiction with their friends, and who use this to build their storytelling muscles and have a fun thing to share with a larger community.

Are there people who go on from writing fanfic to becoming full-time authors? Of course there are! I could list several. There are also full-time authors who write fanfic part time as a form of relaxation. It takes the pressure off the writing and helps them remember that writing should be *fun*.

There's no one way to be a writer, and no one way to run a business. There are some prudent practices for the latter, but with some study, experimentation, mindset adjustments, and time, we can figure out what works best for our style and careers.

And for some of us? That might mean figuring out we either don't want a career in writing, or we want an even slower paced career than we first thought.

Or you might be reading this now and champing at the bit to get on the fast track. Good for you! Just remember, if life trips you up, you can always slow down again.

What are you naturally good at? What interests you? What are your favorite ways to connect?

Allow your marketing and business practices flow from that place. Let go of other people's "shoulds."

Some writers love vending at conventions or street fairs and meeting readers face to face.

Some writers like spreadsheets and tracking ad spend.

Some writers like sending out newsletters or connecting in small ways via social networks.

Some writers love using free serial platforms to feed people into their own subscription models where they can forge deeper connections and increase their income, too.

Action: *What sort of marketing do you gravitate toward? What lights your imagination on fire? If you currently feel like you're dragging your feet and complaining, can you shift your goals or change your mindset? How can you make marketing more fun?*

Reader Retention

Connection leads to retention. It doesn't matter what sort of marketer or writer you are. If you aren't finding ways to connect that work for you and your readers, there won't be much there to retain.

Or if you draw someone into your worlds with a free book or story, but don't follow up, making it easy for them to remain connected with you, they'll move on to the next thing.

If you are a writer who loves automated email sequences, make sure you're building in content and opportunities that capture the reader's interest and imagination.

If you are a writer who loves social networking sites, make sure that your regular posts are offering readers and potential readers a lens into what is important to you. And that includes your books!

Sometimes I get so invested in connecting and sharing—doing my content marketing—I don't do enough *active* marketing. By active marketing, I mean posting something from my catalog of books on a weekly rotation. But that's okay. We all have areas that need work, don't we?

The main thing I've found is that writers who discover an authentic way to connect to readers tend to do the best at building overall goodwill, which helps in the long run. It's not necessarily the best tactic for getting rich quick, but it is a sound strategy for the slow, steady build. This is one reason Kickstarter works well for me: I've built up goodwill that makes people want to share my work and back my campaigns.

Author Michaelbrent Collings talked about this on episode 413 of the Self-Publishing Podcast. He spends so much time cultivating friendly relationships with readers and other authors that people go out of their way to help him, boost his material, and buy his books. They even buy his books in genres they never read! All because he has touched their lives somehow.

Yes, this multi-genre author who started out writing horror...touches people's lives. Don't think that connecting and retaining readers is the purview of one type of author or genre.

Through finding our own authenticity, we find our voice. Through finding our voice, we find our people.

And they find us. All of this is done through a possibility and success mindset.

If we continue to open pathways for engagement, and foster a sense of belonging, a lot of those people will stick around.

. . .

Action: *Take time right now to brainstorm different ways you might connect with readers. Assess how things are going once a quarter or twice a year.*

And don't forget to experiment with creative ways to connect that foster a sense of belonging. That helps with retention.

17

DISCOVERABILITY

Discoverability, for me, is all about finding ways to connect with readers. But I have to find the ways that work for me. You do, too. What works for a thriller writer won't work for a sweet romance author. What works for an extrovert won't work for an introvert. What works for someone in an exclusive program—like Kindle Unlimited—won't work well for someone who is doing direct sales.

There's a classic term from old school marketing called the "seven touches." The theory is that someone needs to see a brand name seven times before they buy. So, it stands to reason that until you have between seven and twenty-seven books out, and have a newsletter, and join multi-author promotions, and have an active presence on a couple of social networking sites...your rate of discoverability will be quite low.

A common mistake early authors make is thinking they can advertise their way out of this by throwing money at the problem and bombarding people with their first—or second, or third—book. Surely, lightning will strike, and my debut novel will skyrocket! Then, something-mumble-something, not-a-plan. Then, riches shall be mine!

That happens. Occasionally. But truly? That happens almost never. As reported during the big Penguin/Random House, Simon and Schuster trial in 2022, most traditionally published books sell around a dozen copies. That alone should show us that advertising a single book does not work. Especially not in a crowded market like we have now in the Golden Age of Indie Publishing.

What does work? Building our catalog. Writing more. We're writers first, marketers later.

Building our catalog builds readers, one at a time. The more books we have out, the more our name is floating through the marketplace.

Yes, here we go again: The best form of discoverability is to write the next book.

I can use myself as an example. When I returned to writing fiction, my three traditionally published books were all that would come up in a search. These days? My fiction far outstrips those books and I have a lot more discoverability as a novelist now.

There are also many other ways for readers to discover my writing: via Kickstarter, Patreon, my newsletter, social media, my website, libraries, and on as many retail platforms as I can get my books onto.

Leveraging those seven touches gets easier and easier over time. The more avenues of discovery we open, the more things like paid advertising can actually work.

Advertising or Marketing?

. . .

Though some people use these terms interchangeably, advertising is a subset of marketing.

Advertising is literally paid ads in magazines or on social media, or an airplane dragging a banner that reads "buy my book" across the sky.

Marketing is pretty much everything else: Your book covers are marketing. Your jacket blurbs are marketing. Your titles are marketing. The teaser at the end of your novel is marketing. What you put in the back matter of your books is marketing.

Every social media post you make is marketing. Each newsletter you send out is marketing. And I'm not talking about asking people to buy your book! What you choose to put out into the world telegraphs a sliver of your essence, causing people to pay attention, to get drawn in, or to recoil.

I know I've bought books because I enjoyed a writer's overall social media presence. And I'm not the only one.

. . .

Marketing as Connection

What changed my attitude about advertising and marketing was realizing that for me, marketing is all about building trust and making connections. Those "seven touches" are all attempts to connect with potential readers. Our social media posts are attempts to build trust, connect with our current readers, and should hopefully be welcoming to potential readers as well.

Whether you're paying for ads, doing content marketing, or posting photos of your cat, ask yourself, "How am I connecting to readers?"

My own writing career is idiosyncratic, and my marketing reflects this. I want to sell books, but more than that, I want to foster goodwill with the people I'm connecting with. This serves me well with things like direct sales. When it comes time to run another Kickstarter, there is a river of people who want to help me because they appreciate my daily posts or my weekly musings.

When I first opened a bookstore on my website, I told no one. Imagine my surprise when I began getting sales anyway. How did this happen? Once or twice a month, I post a short story or essay on my blog, and link to that in my newsletter. People drop by my website to read the story or essay, and then...some of them click on my books.

Because they came from a sense of connection, all those direct sales cost me was some time. As my store expands, my non-organic marketing will, too.

If you are a Lane writer, what works for you will likely be quite different. You're probably better served by posting and sharing only things directly related to your books. A character's favorite chocolate bar. Wizard or dragon pictures if you write that type of fantasy. Support for your local fire brigade if you write firefighter romance. The latest thriller you've read...

Our marketing strategies will hopefully morph into a combination of what comes naturally to us and what our readers enjoy. Over time, those two will merge, because what our readers like is our writing, aka, us!

My point is, we all have our best marketing strategy.

We just need to find it.

Some Basics That Work

What are the basics that work for me, that you can adapt to fit your own style?

Studying book covers, fonts, blurbs, and all the rest is daily or weekly work for me. This is simple to do: sign up for Bookbub as a reader, and check the boxes that tell Bookbub what genres you're most interested in. Every day, Bookbub will send a scrollable list of books to your email inbox. Scan those and see which ones attract you. Ask yourself why.

This project should take you five to ten minutes a day. You can scroll book covers and read blurbs while drinking your morning beverage of choice, or while waiting in line at the grocery store. Over time, you'll get used to the patterns and learn how and where to dig more deeply into what works and what does not.

Next is advertising. I use—very limited—advertising in an attempt to connect with casual readers who may have not seen my name before. I might set the first book in my series to free and pay to list that sale in newsletters like Freebooksy, Fussy Librarian, or Bookbub. As a nonexclusive, or wide, author, I'll apply for promotions on Apple, Overdrive, Kobo, and anyplace else that's offering. And now that it's a going concern, I'll run ads on Facebook to drive people to my direct sales web store.

Exclusive and serial platform writers can also use paid advertising to great effect. Many of these writers post regular Facebook or Amazon ads, or use things like TikTok to drive traffic to their books.

Newsletters. Every author needs one. Lane writers, exclusive writers, and data-driven writers are often well served connecting to readers with automation sequences and segmented newsletters. Check out Tammi Labrecque's work on newsletter marketing if this is you.

My own newsletter is a combination of marketing and advertising. Remember, for me, its all about connection. I connect with my readers and fans via their inboxes every Saturday morning, talking about whatever I'm thinking about this week, usually accompanied by a photo I've taken on one of my daily walks.

Then, below a dividing line at the bottom of the short musing, there's a small ad. It could be a one-week book sale, or my latest Kickstarter, or a new release that folks have been waiting for.

I've cultivated my own voice in my newsletter and social media. My readers know what to expect of me by now, idiosyncratic though my public presence sometimes feels. Whenever I begin to feel like I should do marketing like some other, more financially successful writer does, I remind myself that I have tried to do things that way, and it just did not work for me.

Trying to shove my marketing into someone else's pattern not only didn't work, it made me unhappy and stressed. Besides, we never really know another author's numbers, do we?

Recognizing all of this has helped me slowly build a full-time author career. My way of marketing and advertising works for my personality and my values.

How do you find yours?

. . .

EXPERIMENTATION AND STUDY

How do you find out what works for you? Stop looking for a silver bullet or waiting for a lightning strike.

Experiment. Practice marketing the way you practice writing craft.

And most importantly: don't expect to get it right all at once. I've had to figure out what works for me, and am still tweaking, studying, and changing.

The thing is, tweaking, studying, and changing does not need to be an analytical project involving spreadsheets and projections. Unless spreadsheets and projections are your jam, then have at it! You can party with the numbers while the rest of us do other things.

My studying is a regular part of my week now. But I'm not researching intensively, trying to figure out what is going to work. No. My research is much more casual than that. I'll listen to a business podcast on a walk or at the gym. I'll watch a video or read a business-related book over breakfast. I'll check the Wide for the Win group on Circle once a week and see what topics are bubbling up. I'll study Kickstarters and see what's working for writers with very different careers than mine.

Sometimes I make notes, but other times, I just let the information wash over me, and then experiment with what sticks, if it resonates.

You spreadsheet lovers are likely breaking out in hives at my loose methods. That's okay! Geek out with the likes of Bryan Cohen, Jill and Malorie Cooper, and their friends. They're smart, wonderful people building a community of people who love analytics. There's community for you, too!

I firmly believe that we all can figure out what sort of marketing, advertising, and business practices work best for our personalities, our brains, and our careers.

The bad news: building a long-term author career takes patience.

The good news: building a long-term author career is possible.

• • •

ACTION: *Make a one-month commitment to studying or trying one specific marketing tactic. Then see what happens.*

18

FAILURE AND SUCCESS

The Great Re-Frame

I'VE SEEN authors repeatedly ask why their books aren't selling, as if the books themselves are the problem, rather than discoverability. If this is you, I suggest you page back and re-read the Discoverability section.

I closed the short section on marketing and advertising with the suggestion to experiment. This is where failure comes in.

Failure is necessary for success. Some of us

are terrified of failure, and rightly so. We were punished for it as children, perhaps. Or mocked for it later by people who did not have our best interests in mind.

Some of us are frightened of success for very similar reasons. This fear often comes from the same voices that make us fear failure.

Some of us are going to need to work at retraining those voices that were embedded in us during childhood, or that we took on later in life. The first thing I do is ask myself how those voices are trying to keep me mentally or emotionally safe.

Yes. Believe it or not, some of our critical voices want to keep us small because they want to keep us safe. Failing at something might mean punishment. Standing out might mean we become a target for more abuse. Success might mean that people are paying attention to us and sometimes that feels threatening.

These fears can be true even when other parts of ourselves want success so badly we can taste it.

What does failure look and feel like to you?

What does success look and feel like to you?

Are you willing to invest some time making friends with the internal voices and fears that hold you back?

This can be an all-in process, or something you attend to slowly, over time.

The work to shift our relationship to both failure and success begins with noticing. Noticing our thoughts. Noticing any phrases we repeat to ourselves. Noticing the tight feeling in our gut or the tension in our shoulders.

Noticing all of this gives us greater autonomy when internal or external roadblocks arise. Instead of immediately responding to the fear, anxiety, shame, or whatever, we can take a breath and say, "I recognize this pattern or this voice. What is it trying to tell me? And is it useful to listen to that voice right now?"

Simple recognition doesn't make the fear of success or failure go away, but it does help bring us into a state of action rather than reaction. We're not going to change our entire emotional psychology in a day, or even a year, but we can also figure out ways to not let the voices that want to stall us out, puff us up, or keep us small take control.

You'll notice I included "puff us up" in that last paragraph. Self-aggrandizing, over-the-top "plans" can be as much of a stumbling block as feeling we'll never make it. We are setting ourselves up for failure, either way.

Rather than setting ourselves up for failure, let's reframe failure as a learning process, naysaying voices be damned! And while we're at it, let's set some reasonable success metrics for ourselves!

Let's practice:

"I can learn how to do this thing."

"Finishing and publishing a book is success!"

"I want to take a breath and focus on what's next right now."

"I have plenty of time."

"I intend to publish four books next year. Here's what my word count is, and what a flexible schedule looks like."

"For the next six months, I'm working on engaging with readers more directly. Here are three ways...."

"What did I learn from my last experiment? What do I hope to learn from my next experiment?"

. . .

WHAT PHRASES PING FOR YOU, internally? What other phrases might feel more helpful?

Again, you are a different person than I am, with a different career trajectory. All I'm doing here is offering techniques to help us all get through our fears and into greater clarity.

If failure is feedback, so is success. We can learn from both.

ACTION: *Write down your current relationship with failure and success. Write down three things you have learned over the past year. Then write down how you can—or are—applying those lessons.*

19

MIDSTREAM MINDSET

When to Take Stock

ONCE YOU REACH a certain number of books in your catalog—let's say you've completed your first trilogy, or have six books published, or just reached your twentieth or one hundredth publication—it's time to step back and take stock. How are you leveling up on craft? What is your strategy for leveraging these books you've already written?

What can you do with this wealth of creativity?

I'll repeat one word of that last sentence to help you with your mindset: wealth.

Our books are wealth. They are sources of connection, escape, comfort, insight, hope, thrills, and love. That's part of what makes them magic.

So, how do we continue to spread that magic besides writing more?

We figure out how to open multiple income streams and reach a wider variety of audiences.

That's right. Our "audience" is not a monolith. They show up in different places and like slightly different things. As mentioned earlier, I reach people on all retail platforms in ebook and print. Some authors add audio and translation, which are other great income streams for writers already making a decent income. Some authors put audio up on YouTube or as podcasts—building still more income streams.

But that's not all. There are direct sales, both on our websites and via platforms like Kickstarter or Indiegogo (and Backerkit and the like). Direct sales audiences are quite different from retail browsers. They are not bargain-basement hunters. They often like special editions, or they just want to support creative people.

I can leverage a novel—or nonfiction work—on Kickstarter with exclusive hardcover editions, or extra commentary, or short stories, or art, or a companion oracle deck, or coloring pages, pins, T-shirts, recipes...whatever I think an audience may want. The fun with this is that it allows for multiple audience entry points and forms of connection as well as building income streams.

Some authors leverage books by offering serials and subscriptions. Other authors put together fancy book boxes for their hardcore fans. Some offer omnibus editions or tie-in novellas sold only from their websites.

There are almost as many ways to reach readers and use our story catalog as there are author opinions. Well. Maybe not quite that many, but you take my point.

What interests you? What are you willing to experiment with?

The Midlist Mindset expands our ability to think about our options. We are no longer thinking small and staying in our narrow slots our fears tell us to. The Midlist—and beyond!—Mindset encourages us to think expansively. Would you and your readers enjoy a dedicated Discord server to talk all things books? Do your characters knit to relax after a bouts of fighting evildoers? As part of your Patreon or Ream or website membership, can you offer a tier that includes a monthly online knitting meeting and talk about your favorite books?

As independent authors, we can try out infinite tactics to feed into our overall strategies of reaching readers and increasing income.

A limiting mindset is thinking that to be "real" writers, we must only sell books on official retailers in order to earn our bread. The income that keeps my business afloat may come from a variety of streams, but the source is always the same: I offer up my creativity, my thoughts, and my words in a wide variety of forms. People give me money for it. They write me emails. They tell their friends.

Expansive Mindset Shift

. . .

I'LL GIVE you one example of a mindset shift that works for me, my personality, my energy levels, and my audience: I learned to trust my inner voice around business.

I used to pay for an expensive newsletter service that had all the things that are considered marketing best practices. It offered list segmentation, automated email sequences, audience tracking, and a lot more. I set it all up diligently and onboarded people with a short story and an automated follow-up sequence.

And then I never really used it. This sort of marketing does not work for me. At all. Some people *love* it. If you're a data-driven person, or a Lane writer, this type of newsletter might work very well for you, and for the career you are building.

As a Highway writer, what did I do instead? I stopped paying $500 a month for this service that was useless for me and joined Substack (though I've since switched for ethical reasons). It was free, and simple. I started writing a short, weekly musing with an "ad" below a line break at the bottom.

My open rates and engagement skyrocketed.

That, plus the decrease in business expenses was enough to make me very happy. My personality and marketing style did not mesh well with the "best newsletter practices" that work great for other authors. I can't leverage things that way, or not without a lot of effort.

I offered my newsletter for free or for five dollars a month, using the exact same content. After around a year, I offered my paid members Sprint With Me Saturdays once a month. We get together and chat in between creativity sprints. My Patreon supporters get that, as well. Anywhere from five to a dozen people show up for these, with music, knitting, painting, writing, or even coding projects to work on. That's a tiny fraction of my subscriber base, and totally worth it.

What's funny is, when I began leveraging my newsletter in this way in 2020, other authors were confused or even aghast because I was breaking with conventional wisdom. Three years later, more and more authors are trying out similar routes with great success. Being ahead of the curve hasn't always worked well for me, but this time it paid off.

These days, reader engagement is my favorite

thing about my newsletter. And adding a book or Kickstarter campaign after a line break each week is easy and free advertising for me.

But an amazing thing about my newsletter? As of this writing, I bring in several thousand dollars a year from something I offer for free. I'm happy with this income stream.

This would never have happened if I had not taken a risk away from other people's best practices to find my own.

In future, I may experiment with running my newsletter and subscriptions directly from my website or going back to a regular newsletter provider now that they're catching on to the idea of monetization. I keep these options on the back burner because I know that I enjoy this sort of engagement, and my audience does, too.

I'm ready to pivot as the landscape changes.

Highlighting Our Strengths

So many of us don't fit into "ordinary" categories. Some of us might have a harder time joining newsletter swaps with authors of, say, fantasy romance, because we aren't "Lane" writers who craft stories that hit every trope right down the middle.

That is okay. There are plenty of writers who can take part in these sorts of promotions. Heck, I even join them sometimes if I think my books are close enough that someone might take an interest.

Mostly, though? I find other promotions to join. Ones with themes that fit the mood or characters of my books. I do well with LGBTQ promotions, for example, because readers who enjoy queer characters tend to enjoy my books.

In other words: we can filter and adapt the advice that comes our way, but more importantly, we can lean into our strengths.

For me, this also means leaning into what I think of as my weird.

I'm neurodiverse, genderqueer, interested in magic and justice, and love diverse casts of characters. That's a powerful combo *if I allow it to be.*

And that's where mindset comes in again.

I could allow myself to become discouraged, thinking there was no sort of marketing that might work for me, as I am. I might even listen to advice telling me to niche down, write to market, and file the rough edges off my weird.

Yeah. That advice might work for a few people, but it really is not going to work for me.

A defeatist mindset will tell me, "The marketing that works for everyone else is never going to work for me. I'm a failure!"

A success mindset will offer, "What sorts of things can I highlight to attract the sorts of readers I want?" Or "It's Bisexual Visibility Day coming up! I can do a big marketing push featuring my bi characters!"

Neurodivergent writers are seeing success by featuring their neurodivergent characters. Authors with disabilities do the same. I know that when I highlight a character with chronic illness, I get thank-you notes from readers who also have chronic illnesses.

I'd like to use my friend and colleague Michael Warren Lucas. His books—both fiction and nonfiction—are delightfully weird. Michael makes me read books that I otherwise might avoid, because his voice carries over from his writing into his marketing.

Michael will tell people, "Don't sponsor the special $500 edition of this wacky book about orcs!" And you know what? Someone always does anyway.

He calls his Patreon crew his "Patronizers" and uses his sense of humor spiced with a bit of self-deprecation to reach readers directly.

He also posts a daily rat picture. Michael's marketing techniques will not work for most people. They work well enough for him that he makes a good living as a writer.

I'm the same. Sure, I'm an engaging writer, and I make covers that reflect the tone and genre of my novels. But my books are also...strange. So is my marketing.

Enough people enjoy my marketing style so much that they pay money to support my free newsletter and social media posts. None of what I do are considered standard marketing "best practices." Except, my efforts are best practices for me.

So, if you've tested more usual marketing and advertising techniques and they just don't move the needle? It may be time to double down on your weird.

. . .

ACTION: *Allow yourself to creatively brainstorm your ideal career. What do you think your strengths are? What would you like to work on or study? How might you swim with the stream, and when do you need to swim against it?*

20

CHARTING EXCUSES

Saying "I Can't, Because..."

WHAT EXCUSES DO you give for not writing and not publishing? What excuses do you give for not studying business?

As I've said, I've figured out how to write and publish and study business during an out-of-state move, buying a house, my health tanking, a parent dying, and a brain injury and subsequent physical therapy.

It is useful to practice taking breaks in order

to not let our excuses stop us cold. We all need breaks, but overall if we want to write, we must commit to writing.

In my experience, things like so-called "writers block" are often just the result of fear, or a symptom that we're avoiding looking at something. Or it's a byproduct of perfectionism and wanting to do it "right." Occasionally a block means we need to go a different direction. We have to take a breath, pause, and *decide to move ahead*.

The same is true of all aspects of our business. I've learned to approach business with curiosity as an antidote to avoidance or defeat. Instead of being a puppy digging in its feet and refusing to budge, I let myself move forward and explore what is around the corner. I allow myself to learn.

Facing our excuses requires taking a long, hard look at ourselves. Why are we making excuses? Is it fear, laziness, uncertainty, or exhaustion? Asking these questions helps me to figure out when I can learn to do something, and when I need to ask for help. With my brain injury, certain tasks are almost impossible for me. I ask for help with those. But there are so many business and marketing tasks that, in the past, I would have said I loathed or "wasn't good at" that I now enjoy because they offer me a challenge to grow.

Remember, growth mindset tells us we don't have to know it all, now. That natural talent is not the end-all and be-all. Everyone can learn; we just need to show up and try.

ACTION: *Take ten minutes and write down five to ten excuses you can think of for not writing.*

Then list five to ten excuses for not publishing.

Finally, list five to ten excuses for not learning business.

Go on. This page will still be here when you return.

Time, Attention, and Effort

ONCE YOU HAVE your paragraphs or your list, go through each item, one by one.

Are these excuses based in fear? Avoidance?

Inertia? An unwillingness to re-prioritize? An old mindset it's time to retire? Pressure from friends or family who want to keep you safe, or who want you to live a life they understand rather than supporting your dreams? A sudden disaster or life roll?

Can any of these excuses be taken care of by shifting priorities or finding alternative ways to work?

I used to ask my students: "What is at the center of your life?"

If the answer was family, or creativity, or spiritual practice, or...my next question was always, "And how much time do you spend on that?"

You see, if I say that writing is at the center of my life—or I want it to be—and I spend more time watching television than I do writing? Television is the thing that is *actually* central.

If health is one of my central items, I need to spend a goodly amount of time, attention, and effort on rest, exercise, dietary shifts, taking medication, or whatever else goes into that for me.

The specifics of Time, Attention, and Effort will be different for each of us. I can't tell you what your day needs to look like. Only you can.

Once you're done going through your list of excuses, ask yourself: "What do I want to make more central to my life?"

Choose up to three things, but no more. Everything else must fan out around those one to three choices.

In my own life, Service was at the top of my list for a few decades. After my health tanked, it shifted down to around number six, with Health taking number one spot. These days? Service is around number four on my list of importance.

I'm currently in an assessment phase around whether Writing or Business get equal billing, or if Writing takes top billing. But this is conditional. Overall, writing is more important than business, because without the writing, there will be no business. But five years ago, Writing was just under Health, and Business was much further down the list. While getting my health back on track, writing and publishing was about all I could get done in between bouts of brain fog and exhaustion. Same with my brain injury: because I had very limited screen time, writing took precedence after physical therapy and rest.

I'm stretching myself with business these

days, so I'm writing slightly less than I was. That's fine. I have a decent catalog built up and am still publishing steadily. Writing is still central. One thing that makes it more possible to bump business up for the time being is that writing is so much easier and quicker now, after a decade of intense practice.

In other words, writing has turned into play, which is where I want it to be. I've also endeavored to turn business into fun activity. It's amazing what changes when I approach business with curiosity rather than dread.

This week, I ask you to look at your life and make some choices: what one to three things do you want to make of central importance?

How much Time, Attention, and Effort are you willing and able to spend on these important things?

ACTION: *Take time to answer the question: "What do I want to make central to my writing business? What are three ways I commit to accomplishing this?"*

21

FANTASY, REALITY, AND DESIRE

Imagination Leads to Manifestation

YOU HAVE to want to make a career in writing work from a realistic basis.

Dreams and aspirations are important. I think some people don't dream big enough! For the ancient Greeks, imagination was the foundation every creation is built upon. That can include our author and publisher careers.

That said, for years I've worked hard to distinguish between fantasy—or dreams—and desire.

Fantasy and dreams are rooted in the imagination. They are part of what fuel our creativity and should be nurtured. However...it is quite easy to get trapped in fantasy. We become enamored of the bright lights, the big successes, the money rolling in, the adulation of fans, an end to our family's worries about paying the rent. Our dreams will all look slightly different.

I've got a dream of one of my series getting picked up by a streaming service or film studio. And why wouldn't I? It's a great dream. I even know how I would deal with the influx of cash and have taken steps to assure this would be relatively simple for me if one of the nibbles I occasionally get actually makes it all the way into production. Yes, that's one reason I set up a C corporation.

That planning isn't pie in the sky, though. It is taking a wild dream and grounding it in reality.

Long term authors Kristine Kathryn Rusch and Dean Wesley Smith teach writers to plan for both the best- and worst-case scenarios. Too many authors and indie publishers plan for only one or the other, to their detriment. And a large number, I would hazard to guess, plan for neither, just chugging along, sweating things out, taking stabs at random tactics, hoping they pay off.

Our dreams need strategy to move forward. Random tactics with no strategy can be worse than no tactics at all, because of the time, effort, and money wasted on them. On the other hand, if we have a strategy, we can experiment from there. Even things that don't work for us become fuel for learning, assessing, and planning.

Our dreams are grounded, becoming desires.

So, what is desire?

Desire, in my definition, is something I want enough to go after. I don't just sit around and daydream or talk to friends in coffee shops about how great it would be if one of my books took off. That is getting stuck in fantasy.

Instead, I harness my energy and efforts and channel them toward achieving my desires. This takes strategy, tactics, experimentation, and perseverance. A long-term career requires all of this to succeed. As I've said, we all need to figure out what strategies and tactics fit our lives, personalities, and careers.

If I'm not willing to put my energy behind something, it is not a true desire.

Not Going Begging

TRADITIONAL PUBLISHING HAS LEFT many writers with unrealistic expectations and scars. This is true even for those writers who have never been published by large, established houses.

What we call "traditional" publishing came into existence only during a narrow window of the twentieth century. It's fading now, but we still feel its effects. Traditional publishing—and agents, and predatory contracts, and all the rest—served to make writers feel as if we were beggars holding out a bowl, hoping someone would rain coins and attention on us.

We forgot that we were the ones in charge.

This attitude was thrown into stark relief at one writer's business conference I attended where a representative of the Licensing Expo was present and asked us to role play interactions with companies who might want to license our stories and worlds. Every single author tried to sell the company representatives on their work.

The Expo rep was completely confused and stopped us. "You're the one with something to offer here. They should be selling their company to you."

We were all gobsmacked. Not one of us had even realized how deeply we'd internalized putting others in charge of our work, and our dreams.

We all needed a mindset shift, desperately.

The Mindset Toward Autonomy

My colleague, writer Ron Collins, coined a new phrase for what we commonly call traditional publishing. He calls it "dependent" publishing instead of "independent" publishing. I like that, because it more accurately reflects what writers want from a publishing house: someone to take care of them. These writers erroneously feel that a publishing house will take care of not only editing, cover design, and production, but also things like marketing, all for the low, low fee of ninety percent of cover price.

This just isn't true. It was not true when I was traditionally published, and is even less true now, with a few exceptions. Before Penguin took on my first published book, I had to prove I had a "platform" but was given no support in how to build one. This was before social media became the massive presence it currently is in our lives—though as I write this, social media is once again going through another change, splintering rather than consolidating—and it was more difficult to reach people en masse.

So, how did I prove my "platform"? I had students that I was already traveling to teach, there were conferences I'd taught at, and Yahoo groups I was a member of. Yes, Yahoo groups, which are now defunct.

My platform was not nearly as large as it is today, and I had a newsletter I didn't really use, nor did that first publisher, and the publisher of my next two nonfiction books, have a clue that I even *should* be using my newsletter. Talking with writers who are currently with traditional publishing houses, they've wised up since then.

Back in 2004, the marketing opportunities that were sourced for me by my big New York publisher were neither very good nor very effective. What was effective was everything I slowly learned to do on my own to reach readers. Sure, the publisher paid for endcap placement at Barnes and Noble, but that was really the only thing they could do for me that I could not do for myself.

It took independent—rather than dependent—publishing to help me turn my mindset toward one of autonomy. I'll never forget the first time I met indie author powerhouse Joanna Penn at a tiny authors' business class on the Oregon Coast somewhere around 2016. She asked about my newsletter. I replied that I had over ten thousand Facebook followers and she looked at me as if I had lost the plot.

Turns out I *had* lost the plot! In becoming dependent on my two "traditional" publishers, I had failed to recognize the ways in which I was selling myself short. I rectified this over subsequent years, doubling down on learning what I needed to in order to run a successful publishing company on my own.

This is both harder and easier than you may think.

The move toward a mindset of independence is done one phase at a time. We don't have to learn or apply everything all at once. Remember, to build a successful career, we want to be in it for the long haul. That takes patience, curiosity, and a willingness to experiment, fail, and figure out what works.

Curiosity and a certain amount of patience serve any entrepreneur well because the industry will always change. We must learn to adapt to the changes. This is another reason I prefer independent publishing: as a small company, I am nimble and can adapt as quickly or slowly as I makes sense for my current conditions. The larger the company, the more it becomes like a large ocean liner, slow to stop, and slower to turn.

Remember that statistic about new business success? That it most often takes three years to make *any* profit and up to ten to become sustainably profitable?

If we take this to heart, we can work on building the correct way. Our way.

What Do We Desire?

If someone were to ask you about writing and your publishing business, how would you answer the following question: What do you really want?

No matter what phase you are at in your career, take a breath and let the question sink in.

What do you really want?

What is your biggest writing or publishing dream? What accommodations are you making in case it comes to pass?

What is a scaled-back version of this dream? What feels like something you desire for yourself that you may be able to take solid steps to accomplish?

For me, the biggest dream is the Hollywood or gaming deal. I've already talked about some steps I've taken to make space for this to happen: I set up a C corporation in the US, hired an accountant who understands taxes for creatives, and made sure I can quickly transfer a big influx of money should it arrive. I've also spent time studying from writers who have more experience with film, television, and gaming, and know what lawyer I'll contact should the day arrive.

And when I get the occasional nibble from a Hollywood, or Hollywood-adjacent person, I know how to respond. It hasn't happened often yet, but it has happened. I'm glad to be prepared.

Then, all of that done, I've let the dream go. It is not something I push as realistic because, other than my current preparations, a streaming deal is mostly out of my control. Maybe it will happen, maybe it won't. That is fine, because I have other dreams to foster that *are* in my control.

My basic desire is something that may feel like a pipe dream for a newer writer, but for me, it is something I knew I could accomplish with enough study, effort, and time. And a dash of luck, of course!

I wanted to continue to be self-employed and to primarily make a living with my writing. Now, I already had many years of practice being self-employed, so that part did not scare me. However, the professional full-time writing business is different from my former career, despite that career circling around my three traditionally published books.

Years ago, I had given up the dream of being a full-time writer, because I kept saying I was going to get back to writing fiction and never did. I decided it was a fantasy and not truly a desire. But then two characters appeared in my head and I became excited by storytelling once again. I sought out teachers and a community of people striving to learn business and improve their craft.

Once I decided to re-commit, becoming a career writer turned into a desire. I harnessed my energy, attention, and time toward that aim, studying craft and business, and writing as much as I could, through many ups and downs.

My younger self had a fantasy. My older self transmuted that fantasy—that dream—into actionable desire.

ACTION: *It's time to get real with yourself. What are your writing and publishing dreams or fantasies?*

What are your writing and publishing desires? What actions are you willing to take to make your desires a reality?

What mindset shift will you start working on? What one action will you take today?

22

GAUGING OUR ENERGY

What Feeds You?

As I've mentioned, my career before becoming a full-time author included traveling the world teaching. One thing I *still* teach is to gauge what energy all my tasks, commitments, or strategies require.

We need to commit to ourselves, our writing, and our businesses if our goal is to be in this long term. All commitments can grow difficult over time. Challenges arise. Things change. We need to learn new skills. That is fine.

Every business or job has aspects we like less than others. That is also fine.

So, what am I talking about here? The thing I always ask my current coaching clients or former students is this: Overall, does this commitment feed, drain, or eat your energy? We can apply this gauge to relationships, business, hobbies, volunteering, or any other activity. But for our purposes, of course, we're going to use this to gauge our relationship to our writing and our publishing business.

Before I expand on these definitions, I'd like to remind us that this is an *overall* gauge. We'll all have low-energy days, times when we feel discouraged, or days that feel as if we're Sisyphus, rolling a big rock up a hill. This is especially true for writers with mental health challenges, chronic illness, or any life condition that can feel debilitating.

So, with that lens of overall relationship to our writing and business commitments, let's look at feeding, draining, and eating of energy. After reading through this section, some of us may feel called to revisit the Toxic People section, too.

Let's begin:

When an activity—writing, business—feeds our energy, it means it fills us up. We feel better when we write. Writing infuses us with energy or a sense of joy. Business feels interesting and engaging.

When writing or business consistently drains our energy, it means that we are left enervated or lethargic and have nothing left to give. This is often a slow bleed that creeps up on us over time.

When the activity we've committed to eats our energy, it is often a sign that we've tipped over into a frenetic or obsessive rush and become trapped there. Hustle culture is a big cultural expression of this sort of frenzied mindset, where we feel we must always be on the go, or else we'll fail.

That can leave us feeling like a burnt husk, completely tapped out. People who are engaged in an energy-eating activity often race and race until they completely crash.

Writing should feed our energy. As soon as it starts to drain or eat our energy, we need to assess what has gone awry. Perhaps we need more sleep, or some dietary or exercise changes. Maybe we need a therapist or to change our medication. Perhaps our home dynamic needs a shift. Or maybe we need to schedule shorter writing sprints. We might also need to practice slowing down or changing our priorities.

Business is the same. If it consistently leaves us feeling drained, exhausted, or frantic and overwhelmed, perhaps we need to change up some of our habits.

We could try working in small, delineated chunks of time, instead of trying to muscle through everything all at once. We might sit down and figure out what sorts of business tools could automate some of the load. And for some of us? It might be time to hire a part-time assistant. We may also need to take a hard look at our priorities here, as well.

Not everything has to happen at once.

Thinking long term about our writing careers can helps us find a more sustainable pace and practices that leave us feeling fed.

And again, by feeling fed, I mean overall. We all have times when we need a break, or feel uninspired, or as if our career is *work* instead of something we enjoy. That is natural. Life ebbs and flows.

If you are a writer who also has something like clinical depression or chronic fatigue, you'll need to learn your brain and body well enough to find the patterns of work that best support you. I've certainly needed to do this with both my autoimmune disorder and my brain injury.

You can ask yourself, "Is this feeling coming from my particular brain or body condition, or does it feel different from that? Do I just need a break today, or do I need to pivot overall?"

Everyone can ask the above questions, of course, because we all have different life conditions, but those assessing questions are particularly useful for those of us who have different needs.

If I'm committing to writing and publishing long term, I want to set myself up for overall success. Paying attention to how well our energy and attitude are being fed by our chosen creative outlet ensures that we can continue to show up for writing, and business, and all the rest of it.

If you can't find anything that feels interesting or exciting, overall, perhaps it is time to reassess some of your habits and systems. For example, you could try writing something different, not in the same series. Write a short story in a completely different genre and see what happens. Listen to a podcast you haven't heard before. What ideas does it spark? Read a new-to-you author. What can you learn?

Changing things up in small ways is often all the remedy we need. If larger structural changes are called for, find a way to work on that one small step at a time.

You've got this.

ACTION: *Over the course of the next month, notice how often you feel excited about writing. Notice what parts of business interest you right now. Notice what leaves you feeling drained or burned to a crisp. What can you put more time into? What can you cut away?*

23

WHAT IS YOUR WRITING PACE?

How Quickly Do You Write?

A KEY PART of building your author business is figuring out what your average word count per hour is. Without this number, setting a production schedule is impossible.

This is why professional writers are not muse-driven. Professional writers are craftspeople. They schedule time to write and then they...write.

That is a powerful use of mindset. For a full-time, professional writer, writing is not a precious, rare thing that must be waited for, complained about, or sweated over. Writing is a task like any other, and the more we engage with it, the easier it should become.

Whether you begin your author journey by writing thirty minutes every morning, with an extra hour on Saturdays, or in fifteen-minute chunks while picking up your children from soccer practice or waiting for the dentist doesn't matter. What matters is that you prioritize your writing time.

Most professional writers write at least five days a week and one thousand words a day minimum. Some people write seven days a week. Some people write five thousand words a day or more. The other thing most full-time professional writers have in common? They don't sweat and labor over multiple drafts.

Laboring over drafts only slows you down and rarely makes your book better. When we labor over drafts, we are working from our critical brains, and not our creative brains. When we write with our creative brain, we more easily enter flow. Flow state means more words and better story. This is true for both outliners and discovery writers.

What helps us achieve this desired state? We write more and finish what we write. We let go of finding the perfect plot point or the correct word. We drop into our character's head, open ourselves to what they are hearing, seeing, feeling, tasting...and go.

Word Count Per Hour

How do you figure out your words per hour? Time yourself for twenty minutes. On a slow day when my brain is foggy, I might get three hundred words in twenty minutes. But when I'm in the flow? I can write six hundred words in twenty minutes. My standard pace is twelve hundred words per hour, and that includes five-minute breaks between sprints. Sometimes I write more words in that time, and sometimes less. We could average that out by saying I write one thousand words per hour, which is typical for many writers.

I work seven days a week. As said previously, given the vagaries of my autoimmune disorder, some days I work for an hour or two, while other days I work six to eight hours. I don't count meal or exercise breaks into those hours. That's me writing, marketing, studying, or taking care of other work tasks. I also have a small, related business coaching clients which is a very small percentage of both my work time and income.

Mostly, I make my living with putting words down.

So, back to word count:

If you work a day job and have thirty minutes to write on weekdays and an hour or so a day on weekends, and you write approximately one thousand words an hour, you could aim for a steady five thousand words per week.

What genre do you write in? If you're writing epic fantasy, your books will be eighty thousand words on the short end, and one hundred thirty thousand words or more on the long end. If you write paranormal cozy mystery, your books could be as short as forty thousand words each. Figure out the average range for your genre and aim to write on the lower end of that range, unless you are able to put a lot of time in the chair, typing.

If you are typing five thousand words a week, and your average novel length is eighty thousand words? It should take you four months to write a draft. Let's say you do an editing pass over the course of two weeks, then send that book to a first reader. They get it back to you in another week. You go over their notes that fourth week. Then the book goes off to a professional editor, then gets formatted, covered, and put up on Kickstarter or published on retailers.

This means that if you're writing eighty-thousand-word novels part time, you should be able to publish two books per year. If you were writing forty-thousand-word novels, that's four books a year.

What would happen if you increased your writing time from five hours a week to seven? Or ten? Or fourteen? Play around with the math and see.

Making money at writing is literally a numbers game. The more hours you spend in the chair, typing, the more words you have. The shorter your books are, the more books you have.

The more books you have, the greater your discoverability, and the more fruitful any marketing efforts become. The more books you have, the easier it is to connect with readers.

I want to repeat that: the more books you have, the easier it is to connect with readers. Plus, you're becoming a better writer because more time writing means more *practice* writing. Skill increases with practice.

Next, we ask: How long should a novel be? A novel can be anywhere between forty thousand words and three hundred thousand. Some writers do quite well with writing novellas between twenty thousand and thirty-five thousand words. Ever heard of *A Christmas Carol*, or *Of Mice and Men*?

Personally, I like to write short. This also matches my reading patterns. If you like to read sprawling, epic, two hundred thousand word each books, you may gravitate toward writing that length. Just know that these books can be harder to market, especially these days, when human attention span has decreased. For my alt-history, urban fantasy series, I set a seventy-five thousand range. My regular urban fantasy series? Fifty-five thousand words each. My romantic fantasy adventure trilogy is around eighty-five thousand words each. My two paranormal cozy mystery series come in at around forty to forty-five thousand words per book, like potato chips, or little pieces of bingeable candy.

I also have a cozy fantasy novella series about a mouse and a gang of do-gooding criminals. I ran a Kickstarter campaign to launch those two wee books and it far outstripped my expectations, raising $6000 of revenue. At $3000 each, that is more than many current traditional advances for full novels. Those two wee books will earn more over time, once I put them up for sale on the open market. Turns out, when times are hard, people like short, cozy stories.

What's great about writing this way is, not only can I produce more books than I would otherwise, but I have also internalized the beat structure of my plots, knowing when something needs to happen, or how many try-fail sequences I need in a forty-thousand-word book as opposed to an eighty-thousand-word book.

Internalizing structure in this way also serves to keep me in the flow, which, as I said, improves the story. I can give my characters free rein to play, and discover the story as it unfolds, without meandering or needing to cut a bunch of unnecessary plot lines or side quests because I know what length I'm aiming for.

ACTION: *Set a timer and type for ten minutes. How many words did you type? Set a timer and type for twenty minutes. How many words did you type? Now multiply the twenty-minute section to extrapolate that into words per hour.*

The ten-minute chunk was both a warmup and to show you how much you can get done waiting for an oil change or while picking kids up from school.

Writing Long

BUT THORN, let's take a step back here. What if I'm one of those people who likes nothing more than reading and writing big books?

Figure out what pace works for you. Are you a Lindsay Buroker, who can easily write five to ten thousand words every day? Great. How many long books a year is that for you?

Or are you a person with a full-time day job, a couple of kids, a dog, and the ability to write five thousand words a week? It's going to take you eight months minimum to write a one hundred- and fifty-thousand-word book. Take a good hard look at that and figure out what sort of career you can have.

You'll have some decisions to make. You can decide to slowly build your career so that by the time you are ready to retire, you have a small but decent backlist. That's a great strategy. Or you can find ways to increase your writing time, upping your total weekly word count. Or perhaps you'll figure out something else entirely, like a marketing strategy that engages readers of epic books who don't mind waiting a year between books one, two, and three.

CREATING Serials

. . .

IF YOU ARE one of the "I like long books and I cannot lie" writers, serialization may be a good career choice if you can find a platform that feels like home.

If you're writing serials on Wattpad, Royal Road, or Vella, or subscription platforms like Ream or Patreon, the process I talk about in the section above will look and feel slightly different than if you are publishing complete novels out of the gate.

You'll need to find your own ways to map story structure but could also choose to follow an arc with an approximate word count. Most serial installments are somewhere between one thousand and fifteen hundred words. How long do you think you want to write one particular serial story? A year? Three? How many times a week or month do you intend to publish installments?

Answering those questions will help you set and attain your goals. There are writers making bank on serial sites with sprawling, ongoing story sagas. Other writers garner a small but steady fan base on serials that they then leverage on places like Kickstarter when they feel ready to publish the whole story.

There are likely several other ways to make money writing long sagas that I haven't mentioned. Look around you. Study. Listen to podcasts. What are other authors doing? Do any of those methods appeal to you?

Pick one and give it a year. See what happens.

ACTION: *If you are a long form writer, research three to five ways to generate income from your stories. Which one would you like to try? What mindset shift will help?*

24

BLOCKING OUT TIME

Setting Your Production Schedule

ONCE YOU KNOW your average writing pace and set a schedule that feels sustainable, you can begin plotting out a production schedule.

Why is this important? A production schedule reminds you that you're running a business, not a hobby. A production schedule gives you deadlines to aim for, and clearly shows you when you're on or off track. It also allows you to adjust when life events happen, personally or globally.

We can't deviate from or alter a plan that doesn't exist.

Writers without a production schedule have a harder time gaining traction in their careers. They might write a lot, and never publish, stockpiling work after work for some nebulous future. Or they might have trouble getting to the writing, because there's no missed deadline if they don't. Or they flit from project to project, never building anything.

So, this is another way setting a production schedule is an asset: a production schedule will help you figure out if you want to be a career writer or not.

After tinkering with possible production schedules, some writers will decide to write what they can and publish when they can, quietly putting books out in the world in a random fashion, simply because they enjoy it. That is a terrific thing to discover about yourself. You can remove the pressure of going full time and just play!

Other writers slowly build their catalog over time, releasing a book or two a year, enjoying their lives and the security of their day jobs. They build their catalog slowly, over the course of ten to thirty years. A clever one or two book a year writer will find ways to build reader excitement, using splashy Kickstarter launches or advertising direct website sales to readers who want exactly those stories!

For equally clever one or two book a year writers, publishing becomes a retirement plan. These writers will start to seriously market only once they've got a couple of series out and use that income to keep building the business. By the time they quit the day job, they have a second income-making venture going. That's another good strategy!

These strategies would not have come to light without setting a production schedule in the first place. Setting a production schedule is a good way to get to know ourselves, what we really want, and how we work best.

In my experience, if you want to be a professional writer and are aiming for full or even solidly part time, a production schedule is necessary.

Some writers finish their books for the year before setting a production schedule for the following year. This means they are doing business tasks for last year's books while writing this year's books.

Similarly, I block out my book publishing schedule a year in advance. I brainstorm what old series I want to write a new book in, which Kickstarter books from the previous year need general release dates in the coming year, what new series I might want to spend some time in, and what can go up for pre-order on my website or all the retail distribution sites.

For the author writing serials, or feeding a subscription platform, a production schedule should include that, too. I'm currently feeding a nonfiction book to my Patreon in monthly drips. A Kickstarter for the finished book is already on my calendar, even though I know that slot may need to change. The set date helps to keep me focused.

As said, I tend to publish six books a year, averaging four novels, filling in the rest with short story collections, nonfiction, or omnibus editions. Right now, I'm slowing down, but over time, may ramp up again. It depends on what holds steady, and what changes.

One thing I've learned about myself is that when I set plans during a "good" period, something always comes up: illness, someone dying, a surprise brain injury, or... In other words, life happens.

I've also seen too many writers get on the twelve novels a year train and burn out badly. It takes some of them years to recover and get back to writing. If they do. Other writers happily write and publish ten or more books a year, with seemingly no problem, year in and year out. But that's a pace that is comfortable for them. It's not them pushing all the time.

And that's key.

Setting a production schedule helps us figure out what *our* sustainable pace is, not what someone else's pace is. I'm not fantasy author Tina Glasneck, web novelist Pirateaba, or romance giants Bella Andre or Lee Savino. I can take inspiration from other authors, but I cannot map my career onto theirs.

After moving further north, I've also come to realize that I love morning light, making spring through summer my most productive writing time. I slow down autumn through winter, when my brain tends to feel foggy at six a.m. instead of alert and raring to go. I've adjusted my writing and production plans accordingly, using winter to primarily work on business tasks and strategies that I don't have the patience for during my highly generative times of year.

I still write during those seasons, just not as much, just as I do business tasks year-round.

If I had never set and adjusted a production schedule, I wouldn't have come to recognize any of this.

ACTION: *Do you have a production schedule? Why? Why not? If you do have a schedule, what adjustments need to be made? What might your ideal schedule look like?*

READER EXPECTATIONS

. . .

SETTING a production schedule also helps us set reader expectations and helps with marketing.

Putting out one book every October is better than putting out a larger number at random. When we publish a book every two or three months, our readers get used to that cadence. Publishing books at random is a good way for readers to forget about us. We cannot expect people to keep track, particularly in this age where so many use e-readers.

When a person reads a paper book, they see the author's name and series title every time they pick it up to read. Someone who uses an e-reader only sees the cover and author name when they begin the book, but each subsequent time, they dive directly into the story. Will they recall the author who wrote the mystery or romance they read a year or two ago? Some might, but many will not.

A steady cadence of publication helps to solve this problem. As I said, readers will know when to look for book announcements or, better yet, if you have a teaser for Book Five at the end of Book Four, complete with a preorder link, a significant portion of readers will click and pay in advance.

A clear publishing schedule helps my creative flow as well. I know which series I plan to play in, and approximately when. I build a lot of flex space into my schedule, because, with illness or random life events, something will always happen to disrupt even the most dedicated writer and publisher.

All of this said, we can allow ourselves to try out and practice setting schedules until we find a pace that works for our lives.

ACTION: *What is the current structure of your production schedule? Or what schedule would you like to try? What production schedule do you think works best for the writer you are and will get your books out into the world?*

LIFE BEFORE SCHEDULING

· · ·

THE GOOD THING for those writers who are not yet full time, and maybe haven't set a solid schedule yet? They can write and release without fanfare, choosing to only announce their books once there are three books out in the series, for example. That way, any reader who finds their work instantly has more to read!

This is also a great use of platforms such as Kickstarter, which I discussed throughout this book. Many author/publishers have discovered how nice it is to not publish into the void. A dozen to a few hundred people buying your book on launch is better than pushing to find a handful of readers in a massive sea of other titles on the major retail sites.

Writers with a steady and frequent publishing schedule may find launching on their website first and then on retailers is the best course of action.

The hardest thing for many writers who are new to the publishing game is patience. The long-gone golden age of traditional publishing lives on in romantic notions of a person's first book skyrocketing them into fame and fortune. First, that rarely happened. Second, even big-name multiple bestselling authors no longer get the money they once did.

The midlist indie author knows this is a long game. I get asked all the time, "My first book just isn't selling. What can I do? What sort of marketing does it need?"

The answers are always the last thing that author wants to hear. The first is something I've mentioned already: "Write the next book." Second is: "Get a website." Third is: "Send out a newsletter regularly, even if it is to five people."

None of this means you can't experiment with one book out! Some newer authors do well with in-person events—or on crowdfunding or serial sites—with one or two books.

The only mindset shift I would encourage here is to not spend a bunch of money on paid advertising early on and to keep writing while you experiment with any marketing you may do.

ACTION: *How many books are currently in your catalog, and in how many different forms (ebook, paperback, hardback, audio, translations...)?*

. . .

Better Off Writing

Mystery writer Scott William Carter came up with something called "the WIBBOW test." WIBBOW stands for "would I be better off writing?" That helps return us to the core of our business. It keeps our focus on success mindset instead of scattered to the winds.

Every time an "ooh, shiny!" marketing or publishing technique comes up—or questions like "should I record my own audio books?" or "should I go to five in-person author events next year?"—asking "would I be better off writing?" helps us make a sound decision.

The answer to the WIBBOW test is usually yes, especially early on. The best thing for a writer's career is a healthy catalog.

Once a writer has an established catalog—even one that seems small—trying out various other marketing and even advertising strategies will bear more fruit and waste a lot less time and money.

How do I know this? I took expensive marketing courses too soon, before I even knew what I should be studying. Not only were those courses too soon to be useful to my career—I just didn't have enough books out to make that sort of marketing worthwhile—it turned out they were not the right sort of marketing for my career anyway.

I don't feel badly about making this costly mistake. It's part of how I learned business, after all. But if I can possibly save someone else some time and money and encourage them to commit to writing and publishing long term, I'm happy to.

There's one aspect of the WIBBOW test that some writers fail at in the opposite direction: they write and write and write and never publish. That can also stall out a person's chances at building a strong midlist career.

ACTION: *How often do you choose to write? What takes you away from writing? What is your current balance between writing and business? Does that feel healthy and sustainable?*

. . .

HEINLEIN'S RULES

PROLIFIC MULTI-GENRE WRITER Dean Wesley Smith first introduced me to Heinlein's Rules. We'll set aside Heinlein's particular brand of sexism and focus instead on a useful piece of advice he left for professional writers, which is this list:

- You Must Write.
- You Must Finish What You Write.
- You Must Refrain From Rewriting (except to editorial demand).
- You Must Put Your Story on the Market.
- You Must Keep Your Story on the Market.

I've removed some of the traditional publishing-based details, but the gist of the rules remains the same. Smith wrote a whole book on Heinlein's Rules if you want to explore them more in depth.

Some people quibble with the "refrain from rewriting" portion of the rules. If that is you, take a good hard look at how much time you are spending on rewrites. Is there a way to streamline this process and free up your creative voice? You'll get more books out of it. I "rewrite," but usually not really.

As a discovery writer, I forge ahead with my story, making notes in a cheap composition notebook on characters and important plot points as I go. I will occasionally sweep back through an earlier section and add details important to the plot that my subconscious just didn't know about when I began writing.

Then I have a first reader look at the book, pointing out any egregious plot holes or things that don't make sense. I go through those notes over the course of an hour or a few days. Then the book goes to my copy editor, and it generally takes me an hour or three to fix any mistakes. Occasionally, I'll hire an expert reader to fill in gaps in my research. I might need to make some changes around that, too.

Is that three or four drafts? You could say so,

but it is not the labored rewriting that I hear so many people complaining about. I would rather be on to the next book, because, for my imagination, that is where the fun is.

For me, "finish what you write" was the key to my learning of craft and to my publishing success. Not finishing was my problem before I abandoned fiction for over a decade.

For other writers, publication is the sticking point. Too many people love the writing, but balk at the publishing part. To paraphrase successful indie writer Tao Wong: if we don't publish, we don't make money.

Look at your current career in the light of Heinlein's Rules and see what you might fine tune. Your method may not look anything like mine, and that is okay.

Just go write.

ACTION: *What part of Heinlein's Rules gives you the most trouble? What will you commit to changing to correct this?*

25

CLAIMING YOUR PATH

What Do You Most Enjoy?

THE PATH to becoming a midlist indie author will be different for each of us. Part of setting our path is looking at our circumstances: how many hours of day job do we work per week? Do we have children? How old are those children? Are we caring for an elder? How much support do we have at home? Are we disabled? Do we have a chronic illness? Are we neurodiverse or neurotypical?

Another part of plotting out a path is uncovering what we most enjoy. We can discover this via intuition or testing, of course, which is what I did.

Other writers have found help and insight from Rebecca Syme's Clifton Strengths for Authors work, or Claire Taylor's Enneagram for Authors books and coaching. Russell Nohelty and Monica Leonelle have developed an "author ecosystem" archetype template that I encountered only halfway through writing this book. It's a useful one, and I recommend you check it out.

This system divides authors into desert, grassland, tundra, forest, and aquatic. Each ecosystem has its own strengths and coming to understand those natural strengths can also help us mix in things we may be missing.

I came to my own understanding of this a few years into my career, when I stopped listening to advice that simply was not working for my personality type. In trying to go all-in on the prevailing wisdom, I was undermining the very facets that make me...me. I was working at cross purposes to my strengths.

When I listened to Russell and Monica talking about author ecosystems on a podcast, I began to laugh. According to them, I am a "forest" who, early on, was trying to take marketing advice from "deserts." A desert is a high-production writer who gains success by force, overwhelming the market with sheer volume. As a forest—an idiosyncratic person who thrives on reader connection—these techniques were never going to work for me.

Fortunately, I figured this out on my own, as I said, via experience and intuition.

As soon as I decided to double down on what makes me happy, my career took off. Now, it did not take off like a rocket, more like a train, but that works for me. My career has steadily built, in income, readership, and overall momentum since I heeded my inner voice.

Fighting our natural tendencies and skills can quickly lead to frustration, disappointment, or burnout. This doesn't mean we can't learn new things; it just means if it always feels as if we're pushing upriver, we should probably find an easier, more enjoyable path.

So, what makes you most happy?

- Do you like writing to trend and figuring out what the hot markets are?
- Do you enjoy writing on certain themes across multiple genres?
- Do you enjoy launching books with a splash?
- Do you love tinkering with spreadsheets and optimizing marketing and advertising?
- Do you want to build community with your readers?
- Would you prefer to be left alone to just write, write, write?

We examined some of this in my section on marketing as connection. But, while I've long thought of marketing as a way to connect with readers, I now also add in the fact that my marketing must connect with *me*.

ACTION: *Set aside some time this week to make notes on what you most enjoy about writing, marketing, and reaching readers.*

Your Career Is Your Own

THE THING WE CANNOT DO—WHETHER we write shorter or longer books, and whether we're full- or part-time writers—is compare our careers with someone else's. Yes! Look to other writers and indie publishers for inspiration and learning purposes, gleaning what applies. Don't look to other people's careers to provide a map for your own.

When I was regularly attending craft and business workshops on the Oregon Coast, my mentors had a sign hanging on the wall. "You are responsible for your own career," it said. I took that message to heart.

There are things that writers I trust and look to for inspiration do that I try out. To other things, I immediately say "nope!" Figuring this out took time, though. Over the years, I even had to learn how to sift out things that people I respect and trust do—or don't do—and find my own way.

It is good to know *why* I agree or disagree with certain strategies or tactics.

During first few years studying indie publishing, I was prone to following the shiny. I think it is natural to go where the excitement is currently bubbling to see what the fuss is about. Sometimes the fuss is something that is right for me, but most often, it isn't.

There are also non-shiny practices that may be sound, but still don't work for us. Or they may work during one season of our career, but not another. One example for me is tracking word count. That was helpful when I was starting out and needed to figure out my pace. But over time, tracking word count became a source of stress instead of a helper, so I dropped that and began tracking projects instead. Other writers track word count year after year, seeking their personal best. I cheer them on, then finish the project in front of me.

Taking responsibility for our career means that we must get realistic about how we manifest our dreams and desires. In another example, for years, to build the type of career I want, cost-per-click ads to sell books on retailers didn't really work for me, though I'm testing them out again to see how they perform for direct sales on my website. Neither do platforms like TikTok work for me. Those social platforms are all about capturing attention immediately in an ephemeral cycle. Some authors can leverage this because of a combination of their personality, audience, and genre. More power to them!

I mentioned earlier that my few attempts at using TikTok were pitiful. I considered going all in, taking classes, and figuring out how to make it work for me. Luckily, that consideration did not last long before I realized that as I can't even stand to use the platform as a "content consumer" (a phrase I dislike, but here we are), why would it ever work for me as a marketing tool?

For other authors, both cost-per-click ads and TikTok (or whatever will replace it) work amazingly well! Those authors have different personalities, different audiences, and therefore different careers than I do.

This is where indie publishing becomes simultaneously both complex and simple. At its core, it's just another business. A small local restaurant has a different audience and marketing strategy than a global chain. An artist who has licensed her work into mass production has a different career and audience than someone who handcrafts her wares.

The various platforms will come and go. Knowing ourselves will help us adapt.

Taking Charge of Your Career Mindset

We don't have to love every facet of our job, but we can't continuously dread them, either. That's a major mindset shift!

In taking responsibility for my writing and publishing career, I needed to stop complaining about the parts of my job I did not like or felt I was not good at.

We can always learn. Now, learning can take time and energy, I get it. When my chronic illness was at its worst, I hired out book covers because it was all I could do to write the books, go through notes from my editor, and get them published.

But I truly enjoy cover design, so once my health improved, I began to design my own. What did I do while I hired out, though? I studied covers by scrolling through my Bookbub deals of the day emails. I practiced with design software on social media posts and art memes. That way, once I was ready to start in with cover design, I was prepared.

It's the same with any other facet of business. Joanna Penn encourages curiosity in business, and I've taken that to heart while listening to her over the years. Why? Just as the last thing a writer wants is for story creation to become a grind, we don't want business to feel that way, either.

The thing that changed my career around was deciding I needed to enjoy business, as well as writing and creation. Over time, my relationship to business changed, becoming more creative, too.

That did not come naturally to me, and I'd hazard to guess that treating business as play is foreign to at least eighty percent of writers reading this chapter. That's okay. We can all shift our thinking on this.

But how?

I'll tell you a little story. It may even sound familiar to some of you: I had to teach myself how to learn as an adult.

What do I mean? As a smart, precocious child with a domineering, perfectionist, sometimes violent parent, I learned to gravitate toward things I was already "good" at. Getting shouted at for not knowing the flash card answers right away was not a way to instill a love of learning. Instead, I studied what I wanted to, wrote A+ essays a half an hour before class, and coasted on the rest.

When I grew up and realized I had no strategies for assimilating new skills and knowledge, I knew I needed to do something to change that pattern, or court misery and drudgery for the rest of my life.

I invoked curiosity. And if I wanted to learn something, one of the best ways I found was to get a job that would teach me something.

Years later, when it came time to learn how to

run a publishing company, when I started to balk at doing things I wasn't naturally "good" at, I invoked curiosity again. What is interesting about marketing? What is interesting about accounting systems? What sort of business structure suits me, and why?

Also: What formats best help me to learn? For some people, it's watching videos. For others, it is talking with experienced people. Some people learn by reading. Some people learn by doing. Still others learn by some combination of the above.

I'm a researcher. I find it satisfying to dig into study from several different angles and try to do a small amount of business study every day, just as I read novels every day.

In other words: I've found what works for me and am not afraid to change it up when I need to. You can find your best ways to research.

What is one thing that interests you about the business of writing and publishing? How can you leverage that into systems that help you learn more and with some amount of curiosity and joy?

If you can change your business mindset to

one of curiosity and adventure, your chances of success will increase.

ACTION: *What sort of study do you enjoy? What have you been avoiding studying? What is one way can you shift your mindset and pattern around this?*

26

CULTIVATING EASE

Let It Be Easy

WHAT HAS BEEN my biggest mindset shift the past few years? Letting work be easy.

As soon as I notice I'm feeling stressed or tensing up around a task, I say those words to myself: "Let it be easy."

Sometimes, letting it be easy means taking a break to go for a walk, do a household chore, or simply change work tasks. Other times, letting it be easy means that I pause, take a breath, release the building tension, and get back to the task at hand.

Shifting my business mindset from "this is hard, and I don't know what I'm doing" to "look at the cool things I get to learn" has been a major factor in my making a middle class living these days. If I was still in a constant state of struggling against business tasks, I likely would have given up by now. Instead, my attitude has buoyed my career. I run a solid business now and have plans and strategies in place for more learning, experimentation, and growth.

None of this would have been possible if I had kept undermining myself with repetitions of "I can't." Instead of tripping myself up at every turn, I figured out how to let things feel easy.

This is especially important given my minor disabilities. If I have a day where it is impossible to "let it be easy," then I know it is time for a real break. My brain can only do so much big screen time at once, for example. And other days, I'm too foggy to get into the flow of writing.

But I don't decide this ahead of time. It's not a

form of letting myself off the hook, or coddling my fears, or avoidance. No. I always try first. I try to engage with the business task. Or I sit down to write.

If putting a song on repeat in my earbuds and typing a sentence still doesn't get me there? I try switching to a simple business task. If that still doesn't work? I'm taking the rest of the day off.

Without fail, after a "bad" day where I don't get any work done because I simply could not? I plow through a substantial amount of work the following day, accomplishing in a few hours more than I would have in three days of pushing.

When I first started this practice, my "bad" days still often outnumbered my more productive days. This is both because my health and brain had not stabilized yet, and also because it takes time to integrate a new practice. Listening to my body, energy levels, and brain in this way has been a huge boon to my life.

So, how about you? What do you struggle with? What is your response to that struggle?

Are you willing to shift that toward a possibility mindset?

Your phrase doesn't have to be "let it be easy" but I recommend starting with that if nothing else immediately comes to mind.

Work that we choose to do shouldn't feel like drudgery. Leaning in to drudgery only increases it. I learned this years ago, when I went to finish my degree in my late twenties, early thirties. My geology teacher may have been the most boring person on campus. Everyone complained about his class. How did I get through it?

I decided I would learn one thing in every single class. That's how I kept interested and engaged in a situation that was otherwise out of my control. I couldn't control our boring professor, but I could control my attitude.

So, I did.

ACTION: *What attitude do you need to change about business or writing? How can you let it be easy?*

Structuring Your Day

. . .

THERE ARE people who will tell you that you must write every day. This simply is not true. What is true, however, is that the more regularly we write, the easier it becomes. That is why I wanted to bring this conversation under the heading of "let it be easy."

At first, letting things be easy simply is not possible. We have to buck all of the established systems in our lives. We have to retrain our habits. We have to make choices about energy and time. We might have to revisit agreements with friends or families. And the worst thing? We have to overcome inertia. I touched on inertia earlier in this book, but it feels important to bring it back at this juncture.

Again, inertia tells us that a body in motion stays in motion, and a body at rest, stays at rest. This is why daily writing practice is so helpful, because it means we can harness the power of inertia to support, rather than undermine our goals.

The less we write, the more we have to start from scratch, with a cold engine, so to speak. The more we write, the more warmed up we are at the start of every session. This makes diving into a story when we have a spare ten minutes much more possible.

Those of us shifting from part- to full-time writing really need to figure out how to make inertia work for us. I have known so many people who say, "If only I could quit my day job, I would write all the time." The same is true for caretakers of elders or small children. They think that all the time used by their non-writing commitments will suddenly be free, boosting their creativity and business success.

This rarely happens. At least not without concentrated effort to shift old patterns.

What these people often discover is that they wrote and studied more when they had to cram it into small blocks of time. They also discover that they have no idea how to set a work schedule not dictated by forces outside themselves.

All of a sudden, they have too many choices to make about how to spend their time. Choice paralysis is real. Also, it is very easy for a whole host of activities to fill the spaces that have opened by our change in responsibilities.

Unless we choose to fill those spaces ourselves, first. We have to fill them with the things that we say are important to us. And if that is writing and publishing, well, we have to commit to those.

The only way to shift inertia toward our favor is to overcome the inertia that wants us to stay at rest. So, what does "let it be easy" look or feel like in that case?

Whether we are working a full-time job outside of writing or trying to make a full-time writing and publishing career into a success, letting it be easy means figuring out how we want to practice and where we want to experiment. Letting it be easy does mean making a commitment to our writing and our business, but it also means allowing ourselves flexibility as we figure things out. This flexibility will come in handy when we need to pivot in the future, too.

We begin by trying. We begin by saying, "I'm going to get up half an hour earlier or insist on quiet time for half an hour in the evening and settle in to write." Or we begin by setting Tuesday and Thursday evenings to write for one hour. Or, we begin by saying, "The first Saturday of every month, I'm going to work on business tasks for two hours." Or, "I'll write while waiting for the kid's swim practice to finish." Or, "I'll write on the commuter train."

Eventually, we will find our groove. A schedule that works for us will emerge and we can commit to that.

Internal commitment is the bedrock of letting it be easy, because the choice has already been made. The fewer choices we need to make in any given moment, the easier creativity and productivity become. If we know that we're going to write every time we have a spare fifteen minutes while waiting somewhere, instead of scrolling social media, we no longer have to *decide* to write. The decision was made by past us.

And, amazingly, once we've gotten inertia to work in our favor? We usually find more time to write, create, and do business than we thought we had. This is because we've tapped into more energy by practicing and setting aside these chunks of time. The writing and business have, indeed, become easier. Once any task requires less effort to begin, opportunities to begin crop up everywhere!

So, to let it be easy takes more effort at first,

but once the template is set, ease enters the space.

ACTION: *What time works best for your writing practice, research, or doing business tasks? Are you currently in a state of negative or positive inertia? How can you fine-tune this to let it be easy?*

27

YOUR WORK HAS VALUE

Entertainment as an act of service for a weary world.

One bit of possibility mindset, which will be easy for some of us and very difficult for others, is realizing the value of our work.

Stories spark imagination and help us dream what is possible.

Stories remind us—as writer James Baldwin said—that we are not the only people to have this particular experience. We are not alone.

Stories offer comfort during difficult times.

Sometimes, writing can feel like a selfish activity. Mostly, writers sit alone and make stories up, hoping that someday, someone, somewhere, will read them. That we'll make a connection.

And when we enter the world of making a living with our writing, well...it's easy for some of us to think that our chosen profession is not as important as someone who fixes the boiler when it gives up, saves someone's life on an operating table, or helps keep people fed.

I can feel this way sometimes myself. But then I remember the way in which books saved my life. Reading got me through a very difficult childhood. Writing gave me a way to express things I could not speak out loud for fear of retribution. And throughout history, during revolutions and uprisings, the first people killed are often the poets.

Why is that?

Because the poet's words give people courage and a sense of hope.

Some horror writers talk about how reading horror helped get them and their loved ones through unconscionable terror and oppression. Thriller and mystery writers and readers are often trying to make sense of the world. Science fiction and fantasy helps us to imagine worlds that could be if we let them. Historical novels give contemporary context to what was. Romance lets us know that no matter our trials, love will triumph in the end.

We humans are nothing without imagination. Story captures imagination and propels it into new and wondrous places. Stories not only offer an escape from difficulty, but they also seed the ideas that can bring about culture change.

Culture change is a long, ongoing process. An author friend recently reminded me of an art installation by Jorge Méndez Blake. It is a long brick wall, seventy-five feet wide and thirteen feet tall. At the very center bottom is a copy of Kafka's book *The Castle*. The presence of that one slender book changes the shape of the entire wall, causing ripples up and outward.

Every book, story, and poem we write can do the same.

Here's the thing: we never know the effect our writing will have on the world while we are writing it. We may not even know after that work has been published. Sure, sometimes people write us notes that let us know, but think about your own reading. How often have you let an author know what their stories mean to you?

I bet it isn't very often. But I bet you tell your friends about this story that changed your thinking, or tickled your fancy, or touched your heart.

This is the mindset I would like us all to adopt: writing is important, and stories can change lives.

Even if the only life they change is our own, that is important, too.

ACTION: *Write out the sentence "Stories spark imagination and change lives" and post it near your writing space. Let yourself believe.*

28

TO CLOSE

To close this book, I want to remind us that we can do this!

If I can build a career during the years that I moved six hundred miles, settled in a new house, coped with a complete health crash, dealt with my mother's dying process, figured out my neurodiversity, and then got a brain injury that left me completely debilitated and requiring months of physical and occupational therapy, I feel like there's hope for just about anyone.

Let this be a journey.

Journeys take time and presence. Roads

widen and narrow, curve and straighten. We climb hills and descend into valleys. Every piece of terrain requires a slightly different set of skills and attention.

But mostly? The journey requires our desire. That is our guiding light. Our goad. Our inspiration.

No matter what happens in life or our careers, we can continuously choose to return to following the star of our desire.

We may not feel successful every day. We may need a break, or to gather more information, or to practice more skills. We may need to pivot, or even start fresh. But, as in every facet of life, we can return to the path.

Choosing to share our creativity with the world is an important act. The world needs our creativity, our vision, our hope. The world needs us to hold up a mirror to show what is, and to open a window on what may be.

As writers, we hold the power of imagination and possibility.

Let's keep finding ways to share that. No matter what.

Keep breathing. Keep centering. Remember what is important.

I wish you great success!

ACKNOWLEDGMENTS

This one goes out to my Kickstarter supporters! I couldn't have done this project without you.

I also want to thank the Kickstarter for Authors and Wide for the Win groups as well as my mentors and all the other writers who have shared their wisdom and support over the years.

Thanks to Johanna Rothman, Leslie Claire Walker, Gregory Amato, and Bonnie Koenig for feedback on early drafts. And finally, kudos to Dayle Dermatis, my editor, and to everyone who has read my books and stories over the years.

And thanks as always to my household, who understand the weird life of a writer.

BIBLIOGRAPHY AND WEB RESOURCES

- Alliance for Independent Authors plus the *AskALLi* podcast
- Anthea Sharp *Kickstarter for Authors*
- Becca Syme the *Dear Writer* book series and the *Better, Faster Academy* website
- Claire Taylor *Reclaim Your Author Career*
- Dean Wesley Smith *Writing into the Dark*
- Independent Book Publishers Association

- Joanna Penn and Mark Leslie Lefevbre *The Relaxed Author* plus the *Creative Penn* and *Stark Reflections* podcasts
- Joe Solari *Treat Your Writing as a Business*
- Kristine Kathryn Rusch *Writing With Chronic Illness*
- Monica Leonelle and Russell Nohelty *The Author Ecosystem* website and many author business books
- M.L. Buchman *Estate Planning for Authors*
- Michael Lucas *Cashflow for Creators*
- Malorie Cooper *Help! My Facebook Ads Suck*
- Morgana Best *Authors Selling Direct*
- Pierre Alex Jeanty *7 Figure Book Business Blueprint*
- T. Taylor *7 Figure Fiction*
- Tammi Lebrecque *Newsletter Ninja*
- Tao Wong *Marketing Strategy for Authors*
- Tracy Cooper-Posey *The Productive Indie Fiction Writer*

- Zoe York *Romance Your Plan* and *Romance Your Brand*

MIDLIST INDIE MINDSET ACTION ITEMS

Chapter Two:

- **Action:** *Ask yourself: Do I currently have a growth or fixed mindset? Why? What are the clues? And is this mindset consistent in all areas of my life, or only a few?*
- **Action:** *To begin, take a good look at where you are. Write down your skills—e.g., connecting with people, making graphics, a love of spreadsheets, writing good promo copy—and the things you*

naturally gravitate toward. Then write down a few areas you might want to study.
- *Then, write down what success feels like to you, and then write down the next ten steps to help you there. After that? Back up and pay attention to the first step you wrote down.*
- **Action:** *What changes in your life will most help you cultivate an attitude of curiosity and generosity? Spend some time with these questions. Meditate on them. Write your thoughts down.*

Chapter Three:

- **Action:** *What is one mindset adjustment you are willing to work on this week?*
- **Action:** *What might you like your author/publisher career to look like? Write down three examples of what an ideal day would include. Next, figure out if there is anything practical you want to add.*

Chapter Four:

- **Action:** *Do you want to be—or continue to be—a professional writer and independent publisher? What internal shifts can you make to increase your success?*

Chapter Five:

- **Action:** *Where are you currently in your writing and publishing career? Are you writing your first book? Have you published five books? Thirty books? What is one thing you would like to learn about business, right now?*

Chapter Six:

- **Action:** *What do you enjoy most about writing? How can you foster that enjoyment?*
- *Make some time to study craft. Read books, take classes, or just pick a*

technique and spend thirty minutes practicing it a week.

Chapter Seven:

- **Action:** *Are you surrounded by people who feel supportive and celebratory, or by people who are always fearful, negative, or dragging others down? What choices do you need to make around your friends, colleagues, mentors, or peers?*

Chapter Eight:

- **Action**: *How often do you listen to critical voices? What are three changes you can make in your life to let more supportive voices in?*

Chapter Nine:

- **Action:** *What is one thing you can do to better embrace change and invoke beginner's mind?*

Chapter Ten:

- **Action:** *What sort of writer do you think you are naturally? What sort of writer would you like to be? How can you bring these two things closer together?*
And why?

Chapter Eleven:

- **Action:** *Take a good look at your ambitions. How long do you think you can sustain your writing and publishing schedule in order to support those ambitions? What changes can you put in place to help your longevity?*

Chapter Twelve:

- **Action:** *What is your current financial goal regarding writing and publishing? What is one action you can take to help yourself reach that goal?*
- **Action:** *Make a list of your basic recurring expenses, including*

subscriptions, groceries, car payment, rent, phone bill, etc. What percentage of your take home pay is that? Are there any expenses you can cut back on?

Chapter Thirteen:

- **Action:** *Know your own tendencies. If you are an externally motivated person, what do you think would help the most? If you are an internally motivated person, what are you most excited to try?*
- **Action:** *How many income streams do you currently have, including a day job? What is one income stream you can work on adding over the next three months?*
- **Action:** *Have you researched subscription models? Are you already running subscriptions? Take some time and figure out what attracts and what scares you about connecting with readers via subscriptions.*
- Next: *What mindset shift will free you up to have as much success as possible with subscriptions? Or are subscriptions not*

right for you in this moment in your career?

Chapter Fourteen:

- **Action:** *Take a good look at where you are in your career. How many books have you published? How many series do you have in circulation? What markets are you currently tapping? What is your proposed writing and publishing schedule for the next year? The next five years?*
- *Write all of those numbers down, then ask yourself: What is the best next step to support both my business* why *and* how?

Chapter Fifteen:

- **Action:** *Write down one thing you're willing to commit to, today, regarding your writing and publishing career.*

Chapter Sixteen:

- **Action:** *What sort of marketing do you gravitate toward? What lights your imagination on fire? If you currently feel like you're dragging your feet and complaining, can you shift your goals or change your mindset? How can you make marketing more fun?*
- **Action:** *Take time right now to brainstorm different ways you might connect with readers. Assess how things are going once a quarter or twice a year.*

Chapter Seventeen:

- **Action:** *Make a one-month commitment to studying or trying one specific marketing tactic. Then see what happens.*

Chapter Eighteen:

- **Action:** *Write down your current relationship with failure and success. Write down three things you have learned over the past year. Then write* *down how you can—or are—applying those lessons.*

Chapter Nineteen:

- **Action:** *Allow yourself to creatively brainstorm your ideal career. What do you think your strengths are? What would you like to work on or study? How might you swim with the stream, and when do you need to swim against it?*

Chapter Twenty:

- **Action:** *Take ten minutes and write down five to ten excuses you can think of for not writing.*
- *Then list five to ten excuses for not publishing.*
- *Finally, list five to ten excuses for not learning business.*
- **Action:** *Take time to answer the question: "What do I want to make central to my writing business? What are*

three ways I commit to accomplishing this?"

Chapter Twenty-One:

- **Action:** *It's time to get real with yourself. What are your writing and publishing dreams or fantasies? What are your writing and publishing desires? What actions are you willing to take in order to make your desires a reality?*
- *What mindset shift will you start working on? What one action will you take today?*

Chapter Twenty-Two:

- **Action:** *Over the course of the next month, notice how often you feel excited about writing. Notice what parts of business interest you right now.*
- *Notice what leaves you feeling drained or burned to a crisp.*
- *What can you put more time into? What can you cut away?*

Chapter Twenty-Three:

- **Action:** *Set a timer and type for ten minutes. How many words did you type? Set a timer and type for twenty minutes. How many words did you type?*
- *Now multiply the twenty-minute section to extrapolate that into words per hour.*
- **Action:** *If you are a long form writer, research three to five ways to generate income from your stories.*
- *Which one would you like to try?*
- *What mindset shift will help?*

Chapter Twenty-Four:

- **Action:** *Do you have a production schedule? Why? Why not?*
- **Action:** *What is the current structure of your production schedule? Or what schedule would you like to try? What production schedule do you think works best for the writer you are and will get your books out into the world?*

- **Action:** *How many books are currently in your catalog, and in how many different forms (ebook, paperback, hardback, audio, translations...)?*
- **Action:** *How often do you choose to write? What takes you away from writing? What is your current balance between writing and business? Does that feel healthy and sustainable?*
- **Action:** *What part of Heinlein's Rules gives you the most trouble? What will you commit to changing to correct this?*

Chapter Twenty-Five:

- **Action:** *Set aside some time this week to make notes on what you most enjoy about writing, marketing, and reaching readers.*
- **Action:** *What sort of study do you enjoy? What have you been avoiding studying? What is one way can you shift your mindset and pattern around this?*

Chapter Twenty-Six:

- **Action:** *What attitude do you need to change about business or writing? How can you let it be easy?*
- **Action:** *What time works best for your writing practice, research, or doing business tasks? Are you currently in a state of negative or positive inertia? How can you fine-tune this to let it be easy?*

Chapter Twenty-Seven:

- **Action:** *Write out the sentence "Stories spark imagination and change lives" and post it near your writing space. Let yourself believe.*

ABOUT THE AUTHOR

T. Thorn Coyle worked in many strange and diverse occupations before settling in to write books full time.

Author of the *Seashell Cove Paranormal Mystery* series, the *Pride Street Paranormal Cozy Mysteries*, *The Steel Clan Saga*, *The Witches of Portland*, *The Mouse Thief Adventures*, and *The Panther Chronicles*, Thorn's multiple non-fiction books include *Sigil Magic for Writers, Artists & Other Creatives*, *Kissing the Limitless*, *Make Magic of Your Life*, and *Evolutionary Witchcraft*. Thorn's work also appears in many anthologies, magazines, and collections.

An interloper to the Pacific Northwest U.S., Thorn drinks a lot of tea, pays proper tribute to the neighborhood cats, and talks to crows, squirrels, and trees.

Connect with Thorn:
www.thorncoyle.com

ALSO BY T. THORN COYLE

FICTION

Seashell Cove Paranormal Cozy Mysteries

Bookshop Witch

Haunted Witch

Tarot Witch

Running Witch

Hallows Witch

Solstice Witch

The Pride Street Paranormal Cozy Mysteries

Sushi Scandal

Flower Frenzy

Muffin Murder

Hairspray Horror

The Mouse Thief

Mouse's Folly

Mouse's Fight

The Witches of Portland (complete)

By Earth

By Flame

By Wind

By Sea

By Moon

By Sun

By Dusk

By Dark

By Witch's Mark

The Panther Chronicles (Complete)

To Raise a Clenched Fist to the Sky

To Wrest Our Bodies From the Fire

To Drown This Fury in the Sea

To Stand With Power on This Ground

The Steel Clan Saga

We Seek No Kings

We Heed No Laws

We Ride at Night

Short Story Collections

A Hint of Faery

A Touch of Faery

A Spark of Magic

A Flame for Yuletide

A Hope for Winter

A Time for Magic

A Speculation of Stars

A Speculation of Hope

A Speculation of Time

Risk It All: Queer Stories of Love, Suspense, And Daring

Thresholds: Queer Stories of Love, Suspense, And Daring

Ghost Talker

Cats and Other Creatures

NON-FICTION

You are the Spell (late 2024)

Sigil Magic for Writers, Artists, & Other Creatives

Crafting a Daily Practice

Resistance Matters

Evolutionary Witchcraft

Kissing the Limitless

Make Magic of Your Life

www.ingramcontent.com/pod-product-compliance
Lightning Source LLC
Chambersburg PA
CBHW050509240426
43673CB00004B/161